PHOTOVOICE REIMAGINED

Creative Research Methods in Practice

Series Editor: **Helen Kara**, We Research It Ltd.

This dynamic series presents short practical books by and for researchers around the world on how to use creative and innovative research methods from apps to zines. Edited by the leading independent researcher Helen Kara, it is the first series to provide guidance on using creative research methods across all disciplines.

Forthcoming in the series:

Doing Phenomenography: A Practical Guide
By **Amanda Taylor-Beswick** and **Eva Hornung**

Fiction and Research: A Guide to Connecting Stories and Inquiry
By **Becky Tipper** and **Leah Gilman**

Find out more at
bristoluniversitypress.co.uk/
creative-research-methods-in-practice

PHOTOVOICE REIMAGINED

Nicole Brown

With a Foreword by
Laura Lorenz

P

First published in Great Britain in 2024 by

Policy Press, an imprint of
Bristol University Press
University of Bristol
1–9 Old Park Hill
Bristol
BS2 8BB
UK
t: +44 (0)117 374 6645
e: bup-info@bristol.ac.uk

Details of international sales and distribution partners are available at
policy.bristoluniversitypress.co.uk

© Bristol University Press 2024

British Library Cataloguing in Publication Data
A catalogue record for this book is available from the British Library

ISBN 978-1-4473-6937-0 hardcover
ISBN 978-1-4473-6938-7 paperback
ISBN 978-1-4473-6939-4 ePub
ISBN 978-1-4473-6940-0 ePdf

Cover design: Qube Design
Front cover image: iStock/Veronika Oliinyk

To my son, my husband, and my parents, who in their own ways have all taught me that a picture is worth a thousand words.

Contents

List of figures and tables

Figures

Tables

About the author

Nicole Brown works at University College London and London South Bank University, and she is Director of Social Research & Practice and Education Ltd. Nicole's creative and research work relate to physical and material representations of experiences, the generation of knowledge, and research methods and approaches to explore the same. Her publications include *Lived Experiences of Ableism in Academia: Strategies for Inclusion in Higher Education*, *Ableism in Academia: Theorising Experiences of Disabilities and Chronic Illnesses in Higher Education*, *Embodied Inquiry: Research Methods*, *Making the Most of Your Research Journal*, and *Creativity in Education: International Perspectives*. Nicole's creative work has been published in academic journals and non-academic anthologies. Nicole shares her work at www.nicole-brown.co.uk, and she tweets as @ncjbrown and @AbleismAcademia.

Acknowledgements

No book emerges in a vacuum, and every time I finalise a manuscript, I feel indebted and grateful to many. Some will recognise themselves, although others may not actually know of their impact. Such is the inspiration we all gain from interacting and conversing.

In the case of this book, my most heartfelt thanks go first and foremost to Dr Helen Kara. For it was Helen's email outlining her new 'how to' guides for creative research methods that made me think of writing *Photovoice Reimagined*. Once I had a rough idea, Helen's enthusiasm ensured that I saw the process through to the end. Thank you for your support and friendship, Helen.

Thank you to Dr Laura Lorenz. It is always a privilege to be asked to return as a trainer to deliver workshops for Photovoice Worldwide. I would like to take this opportunity to also thank Stephanie Lloyd, Lee Anne Tourigny, Erica Belli, and Julie Sanders from Photovoice Worldwide for their roles in maintaining this fabulous network of people interested in and focused on using photovoice in research. And of course, I am equally grateful to the delegates in my Photovoice Worldwide workshops. Their questions and concerns highlighted what needs to be covered in a 'how to' and so they actively shaped the contents of this book.

I would also like to thank all staff members at Policy Press, from editors, copywriters, typesetters, graphic designers, through to marketing specialists – above all, Paul Stevens. Your belief in the value of a book on photovoice was the encouragement I needed to persevere when the going got tough.

I am always hugely grateful to friends in academia and from the creative industries, who are happily listening to me fleshing out my ideas. These brainstorming sessions are incredibly valuable to me, even if they may bore you all. Special thanks to Dr Amanda Ince, Dr Jo Collins, Dr Agata

Lulkowska, Áine McAllister, and Dr Sara Young, as well as the community of artists around Kent Creative and Creek Creative (www.creek-creative.org) – above all, Nathalie Banaigs, Sue King, and Bob Lamoon. Dr Alison Finch and Alejandra Carles-Tolra (www.alejandractr.com) – I would like to thank you for allowing me to use your work, which has been so influential for my thinking.

Thank you to the photographers Steve Bloom (www.stevebloom.com), Alex Hare (www.alexharephotography.com), Rob Canis (www.robertcanis.com), and Terry Whittaker (www.terrywhittaker.com), whose workshops, presentations, training sessions, and photographs have been inspirational and educational. I feel very privileged to have had the one-to-one time with you. Having had the opportunity to talk about photography has helped me immensely in working through the use of photographs in research contexts.

Finally, I would like to thank my family. My father Seppi, my mother Otti, my husband Craig, and my son Stephen: you all continue to educate me about how to do photography well.

Foreword

Laura Lorenz, PhD, MEd
Co-founder of Photovoice Worldwide
and a Visiting Research Scholar at
Brandeis University, Massachusetts

I met Dr Nicole Brown when she co-presented on a visuo-textual analysis framework for analysing research photos and text at *The Qualitative Report*'s 2020 online conference. Despite the late hour – after midnight for her – Dr Brown's presentation of her iterative framework immediately caught my attention, and I invited her to teach an online workshop series for Photovoice Worldwide. We settled on 'Key Themes in Photovoice Research', a three-workshop series on creative methods for data collection, analysing data from creative methods, and the role of emotions and reflexivity in photovoice research. I have learned much from her teaching and writing.

We see these same topics – data collection, data analysis, and reflexivity – woven into this slim but impactful volume, *Photovoice Reimagined*. Each chapter has aims, an introduction, a chapter body, and end of chapter tasks, and she encourages us to journal as we engage with the content. Photovoice is in essence an experiential or hands-on method. When we ask co-researchers to take photos and make sense of them, they are *doing* photovoice. With the chapter exercises, Brown creates opportunities for us to *do* experiential learning about photovoice as a method and a framework, and apply the learning to our photovoice practice.

Brown is well known for using creative methods of reflexivity to lay bare our preconceptions – of ourselves, our co-researchers, and the meaning of our data. In this book she models taking risks and being vulnerable as she shares the photos and art she has created as part of her own research practice. I encourage you to follow her model and be vulnerable to your photovoice co-researchers as well – to encourage a more authentic and meaningful photovoice experience for all.

This book has reminded me that we must be patient with ourselves and our inevitably imperfect photovoice practice. My facilitation of photovoice has become more participatory over time as I have grown in my understanding about how to better share power with my co-researchers. This book has encouraged me to think about ways to continue to reimagine my photovoice practice, achieve my participation and social change goals, and aim for lasting impact.

By the time you have finished this book, you will understand photovoice as a framework for viewing participation and social change and as a method or way of enacting participation and social change with co-researchers and stakeholders. You will have a more informed view of how your practice fits into a larger participant engagement-social change continuum for participatory visual methods including photovoice. You will better understand your choices for photovoice as a framework and a method, and the imperative of introducing an anticolonial lens into your photovoice practice or of strengthening your existing lens.

In Chapter 1, Brown notes that photovoice and photo elicitation are two sides of the same coin. She reviews the historical foundations of the methods and sets the stage for the rest of the book. She argues that the ability of photographs to show – not tell – leads to new and different understandings. She cautions us to recognise that our preconceptions and misunderstandings can lead to misinterpretation of our co-researchers' capabilities, photos, captions, and interview data.

Chapter 2 proposes viewing photovoice as both a method and framework. With the chapter figures Brown presents a visual way to understand and reflect on our approaches and method choices, with a view towards encouraging maximum participation and transformation of facilitators and co-researchers alike. The continuums inspire us to reflect on and be transparent with ourselves about the personal and professional lenses that influence us – and recognise where we can grow and evolve in our photovoice research practice.

In Chapter 3 the focus is on data collection. Brown discusses photos as data and photos as sense-making. She shares a continuum that challenges readers to locate their data collection approach. Are they interested in the combination of photos and group discussion? The photos or text alone? She argues that context matters, and that we need to adjust our approach to every photovoice project, to better fit its context.

Chapter 4 focuses on approaches to data analysis and acknowledges the challenge that many photovoice researchers struggle with – what data can they interpret? It is long recognised by visual sociologists that researchers and audiences quickly jump to conclusions when looking at a photograph. Brown suggests using journalling and arts-based methods to slow down, see our photovoice data with more thoughtful eyes, and avoid quick interpretations. She encourages involving participants in the analysis process, to increase the accuracy and relevance of photovoice findings.

Chapter 5 is centred on a rapidly evolving aspect of photovoice: dissemination. In this chapter Brown highlights different quality criteria for photos generated using photovoice. She describes the array of potential outreach to effect social change. She discusses the consequences of dissemination and how it can make participants vulnerable to criticism. She notes that dissemination is challenging and requires time, money, skills, and contacts, and that facilitators play an important role in ensuring that dissemination is ethical as well as effective.

The book's final chapter turns a spotlight on photovoice ethics. Brown raises the challenge of designing a participatory research process while gaining approval from a research board – which may require that the entire project be designed and described ahead of time. She reviews photo ownership, asking permission from people being photographed, and the difference between taking photos for personal and research purposes.

With this book Brown encourages us to sustain a continual, relational process with photovoice and our co-researchers. She places responsibility for the transformative potential of photovoice directly on us. The guidance she provides here strengthens our ability to critically examine, envision, and facilitate photovoice research and aim for the positive social change impact that the method's creators, Caroline Wang and Mary Ann Burris, have called for since the inception of photovoice 31 years ago. I encourage you to let this book guide your reimagining of photovoice and your relationship with it for yourself.

How this book can help

This book has been designed as an introductory text to photovoice research to provide guidance on what photovoice research is and how it can be carried out.

In my experience there are two bodies of literatures available in relation to PhotoVoice, photovoice, and photo-elicitation projects, henceforth photovoice. There are the 'how to' books that describe how to do photovoice (for example, Latz, 2017; Jaldorrn, 2019; Breny and McMorrow, 2020); and then there are many articles reporting on studies using photovoice. This second body of literature is sometimes problematic, as aspects of photovoice are often diluted to suit specificities of research contexts and funding. Also, terminologies are invariably ambiguous across the globe, and what may be called 'photovoice' in some contexts will not be recognised as photovoice in others. Additionally, research methods and approaches get confounded, misinterpreted, and misunderstood. And in the case of photovoice I have noted that a blurring with photo-elicitation projects is often the result.

The book I have written, therefore, fulfils a very specific purpose. *Photovoice Reimagined* presents photovoice as a continuum from 'minimal participant engagement, limited social change' to 'maximum participation, active transformation'. Within that continuum then, photovoice is described as a method (encompassing all forms of photo-elicitation work) and as a framework (photovoice in its purest sense). Thus, the original contribution of *Photovoice Reimagined* lies in the reframing of what constitutes photovoice and photo-elicitation projects. This reframing is not meant to confuse, but to enable readers to adjust existing practices for their specific research questions, purposes, settings, and contexts. With this reframing in mind – hence the *Reimagined* in the book title – the book takes you through methodological, practical, and ethical considerations for planning, carrying out, and disseminating your research. In this sense, *Photovoice Reimagined* is itself a methodological toolbox for all phases of research, from which you can deliberately select what is most appropriate. At the same time, *Photovoice Reimagined* asks that you are more consciously aware of and, as a result, more transparent about the choices you make, when you adapt existing approaches.

We all know that the planning and the carrying out of a research project is not ever linear, yet, I have decided to replicate the structure that is so typical in research methods guidebooks. In each chapter I combine examples from literature with my own experiences from research to highlight outline theories, techniques, and strategies related to photovoice research.

The guiding principle underlying this book is that you need to find out for yourself what works for you. You will find that I offer an overview of traditional photovoice research along with reimagining photovoice as a method. These applications of photography may not be sitting within the strictly traditional definition of photovoice, but will expand your methodological toolkit. While I can offer examples and guidance, the final design for and ultimate completion of a photovoice research is highly contextualised and depends on so many factors that I cannot provide that individual support.

You are encouraged to engage with the book through journalling in response to the contents presented and by completing the end of chapter tasks. Your journalling may take the form of taking notes in a journal, once you have undertaken the end of chapter tasks; or you may want to experiment with further creative responses by creating photographs about your experiences in the end of chapter tasks, for example. My hope is that through this engagement you will experience, at least to some extent, what it feels like to be involved in photovoice research, which, in turn, shall make it easier to decide if this is the right research approach for your particular circumstances.

Chapter overviews

In Chapter 1, I provide a historical overview of photovoice and introduce photovoice as a research method. I finish the chapter by outlining the definition of photovoice for the scope of this book.

Chapter 2 addresses the 'how to' of designing photovoice research. I explore the philosophical and theoretical foundations in photovoice research along with potential research foci and questions that photovoice research may investigate, and what roles participants play in that context.

Building on the previous chapters, I reimagine photovoice as a method and as a framework in Chapter 3. That reimagination sees me identify different forms of data collection in photovoice research, and I offer guidance and practical steps of how to collect data in photovoice research.

As Chapter 4 deals with analysis, I begin by demystifying the analysis of photographs in generic terms before moving on to how to analyse photographic data in combination with textual data. I return to the idea of reimagining photovoice by offering guidance on how to create photographs as an analytical process.

In Chapter 5, I focus on dissemination. I do so by reflecting on dissemination as a pathway to impact and by exploring how to assess good quality in photovoice research, before I present some advantages and drawbacks of different ways for disseminating photovoice research.

Chapter 6 is looking backwards and forwards, in that it brings together the missing threads of ethical considerations from the previous chapters with a reflection on how photovoice research may be developed further.

End of chapter tasks are offered as an opportunity to engage with the contents at a practical level. Although the book does not have to be read chronologically, the activities do build upon one another from one chapter to the next to exemplify how a photovoice project may develop gradually and continually.

Colour versions of the photographs in this book are available to view online at:

https://policy.bristoluniversitypress.co.uk/photovoice-reimagined

1

Introducing photovoice

Chapter aims

- To provide a historical overview of photovoice.
- To introduce photovoice as a research method.
- To define photovoice for the scope of this book.

Introduction

Photovoice is a particular approach to research that emerged in the 1990s in response to wider developments within qualitative research. Researchers more formally recognised the power they held in the relationship to their participants and began to feel uncomfortable about the researcher-researched hierarchy. As a result, trends moved towards participatory and creative approaches to minimise these hierarchies, to reduce the power differentials between participants and researchers, and to equalise the responsibility among the stakeholders within the research. In addition, smartphones, tablets, or action cameras have eased availability of and accessibility to relatively cheap and simple means for recording through photography. Where once detailed knowledge of the photographic process may have been required to enable individuals to capture meaningful information and data, editing apps and software further facilitate the development of photography. As a result, research projects employing photographs became more prominent.

Table 1.1: Number of publications relating to photovoice and photo elicitation per decade from 1990 to 2022

Search term	1990–99	2000–09	2010–19	2020–22
Photovoice	136	2,360	16,200	12,600
Photo elicitation	2,270	8,160	17,300	17,100

A quick search on Google Scholar for the key terms 'photovoice' and 'photo elicitation' demonstrates just how significant that change has been over the past 30 years (see Table 1.1).

Articles relating to 'photo elicitation' nearly octupled between the 1990s and the 2010s, whereas articles relating to 'photovoice' multiplied by 120. In the two years between 2020 and 2022 alone, Google Scholar lists 12,600 articles including the search term 'photovoice' and 17,100 articles including 'photo elicitation'. The popularity of research studies using photography as an approach to gathering data is indisputable. However, the terminologies and conceptualisations are not always entirely clear.

Conventionally, photo elicitation relates to an approach within interviewing whereby researchers and/or participants use photographs as a starting point for conversations. The researchers take advantages of photographs as a stimulus to 'elicit' a response from and in their participants. The photographs may be supplied by participants or researchers, but the dominating research approach still remains the interview, thus the conversation between the researcher and the participants. The concept of photovoice, by contrast, builds on the idea that everyone has a unique perspective and voice, and that these voices should be heard and respected.

Traditional research methods, such as interviews, often privilege the voices of those in power and may not accurately represent the experiences and perspectives of marginalised groups. After all, it is the researchers who develop the research question based on their research focus and interest, who ask the interview questions, who analyse the data, and who therefore control the knowledge generation in the research process (see Chen, 2011; Mayorga-Gallo and Hordge-Freeman, 2017; Kaaristo, 2022). Research participants do hold some power, as they decide which information they are willing to share. Yet, often, this is the only power participants hold. Photovoice, however, actively seeks out to hand over the responsibility of the entire research process to the participants. Photovoice asks individuals to visually document their own lives and communities, and to use these images as a starting point for advocacy around the issues that are important to them. One of the key features of photovoice is that this is a fully participatory process. Participants are trained in photography and research skills, and they are encouraged to take photographs that reflect their own experiences and perspectives. The photographs are then used as a catalyst with the participants then collaborating on strategies to address the concerns they have uncovered and documented. These strategies may include creating exhibitions of the photographs, developing educational materials, or advocating for policy change.

The following table (see Table 1.2) should provide further clarity between photovoice and photo elicitation (Brown, 2023, np).

Table 1.2: Overview of photovoice and photo elicitation

	Photovoice	Photo elicitation
What is it?	Photovoice is not truly a data collection method. It is actually a research framework that uses photographs for the purpose of social transformation.	Photo elicitation is an approach to data collection that uses photographs to enhance conventional interviews.
What is its philosophical underpinning?	Photovoice is a feminist, activist, and egalitarian research approach aiming at empowering individuals as well as entire communities, and thereby bringing about change. The photographs are therefore meaningful representations of experiences and data in and of themselves. This means that the photographs are not to aid conversation or stimulate thoughts but are artefacts that are analysed together.	Researchers recognise that interviews may be experienced as uncomfortable, difficult, or even confrontational, and that participants may not fully engage with the research process. The philosophical underpinning for photo elicitation therefore lies with the fact that the photographs may offer 'a way in' to the interview, to home in on participants' thoughts or experiences, and thereby stimulate conversation.

(continued)

Table 1.2: Overview of photovoice and photo elicitation (continued)

	Photovoice	Photo elicitation
Why would you do it?	Photovoice researchers are often activists who are embedded in, or at least serving, particular communities.	Most researchers recognise the benefits of photo elicitation during interviews and are even keen to use photographs in their research reports, as 'a picture is worth a thousand words'.
Why would you not do it?	Photovoice projects are time-consuming and require the participants to be fully engaged in the research process. For many researchers who work to deadlines or grant funding requirements, a true photovoice project is therefore often pragmatically impossible.	Researchers shying away from photo elicitation projects often worry about how to deal with data sets that may be incomplete because some participants have not submitted photographs, or about how to interpret and analyse the visual materials.
How do you do it?	Photovoice in its original delineation follows a specific process that begins with the recruitment of participants and ends with dissemination. Some key steps include: • Selection and recruitment of a target audience of policy makers or community leaders. • Recruitment of a group of photovoice participants. • Arranging for the photovoice research to be carried out. • Planning events and opportunities to connect participants with policy makers or community leaders to act on the proposed recommendations (adapted from Wang, 1999, pp 187–9).	There are different approaches to data collection within photo elicitation studies. In some studies, the researchers provide photographs they think appropriate and conducive for the interviews. In others, which is probably the more common approach, the researchers will ask their participants to supply photographs for the interview. Photographs may either be specifically taken and created for the study, or they may be selected from newspapers, fliers, magazines, and the internet.

While photovoice and photo elicitation initially were two quite distinct approaches to research in the social sciences, the boundaries are more blurred nowadays. In part, this is due to researchers designing projects to suit their specific target communities and target participants, and so adjusting elements of a research method.

In part, this is also due to developments that rendered photovoice and photo elicitation a kind of diary method with communities that would otherwise be difficult to reach. The social-distancing rules that were put in place during the COVID-19 pandemic exacerbated this trend of using photographs as a form of remote data collection. As the approaches along with the terminology have varied over time, many visual methods or forms of visual enquiry have also been used to describe what others define as 'photovoice' or 'photo elicitation'. In order to untangle this web, I sketch out the historical beginnings of photovoice before I outline some of the strengths and weaknesses of photovoice as they have been reported in literature. I conclude this chapter with a reframing of photovoice, which forms the foundational principle for the remainder of this book.

Historical overview of photovoice

The use of photographs in research

Historical developments are notoriously difficult to chart, as demographical, technological, political, cultural, economic, and educational factors impact society as a whole, which in turn influences philosophical outlooks on research as well as research designs and approaches. In addition, as is often the case, concepts and terminologies, definitions are misinterpreted, adapted, and adjusted, which leads to further confusion and conflation. However, the use of photography in research is not new at all. Indeed, photography played a key role as a scientific means to objectively record cultural characteristics, and physical-material differences, specifically in the colonial periods of the late 19th and early 20th century (Pink, 2021). Initially, photographs were an opportunity to record, capture, and document in the context of ethnography and anthropology, especially as part of a positivist research paradigm (for example, Král, 1956; Collier, 1957).

As researchers became more consciously aware of their positionality, of relationships and power dynamics between researchers and participants, participatory approaches gained traction. Worth and Adair's (1972) *Through Navajo Eyes* is particularly noteworthy in this context. The premise of the study was to explore what would happen if a group of people, in this case the Navajo, who have never made films were taught to make films for the first time. The authors outline how they approached the community, offered training sessions on the use of film cameras, and then analysed the outcomes. Their analysis emphasises the cultural-specificity involved in developing films, as we use particular patterns and shots to express ourselves. The films emerging from Worth and Adair's (1972) project not only offer important insights into Navajo life and culture, they also illustrated the immense value of recordings that are made by the community members themselves.

In the wake of Worth and Adair's (1972) seminal work, Smith and Ziller (1977) asked participants to take photographs of their lived experience in three phenomenological studies using photography rather than film as a medium of data generation. One study focused on the relationship between Black and White students, the second study explored the lived experience of disability, and the final study related to the presentation of self among men and women. Similarly, Ximena Bunster (1977) explored 200 working mothers in Lima, Peru, who were illiterate or poorly educated and how these women managed their everyday survival given the significant disadvantage they experienced. These studies continued in the vein of documenting and recording while also beginning to recognise the role of photography as a tool for meaning-making. On this front, Messaris and Gross (1977) and Caldarola (1985), specifically, moved the use of photography within research forward. Both studies focused on and actively employed the contextualised, interpretative nature of photography, when they considered how viewers make sense of the images they are presented with. What stands out with these early research designs is the tendency towards participatory, egalitarian research as well as the recognition that the predominant form of knowledge generation marginalises individuals and particular groups of people. With that came the recognition that images were able to deepen participants' reflections and enabled them to access 'a different part of human consciousness' (Harper, 2002). This power of the image became more formally recognised and gradually became used more deliberately in contexts of therapy, research, and activism (for example, Dowdall and Golden, 1989; Stamps III, 1990).

Photography as empowerment in research

At the same time, the rise of participatory research paradigms, feminist theory, and Freire's (2021) education for empowerment and critical consciousness (see Chapter 2) further impacted trends within social sciences research. Participatory Action Research, in particular, highlighted the need for participants to be actively involved and engaged in the research process from conception through to dissemination (Tandon, 1988). While the achievement and impact of Worth and Adair's (1972) research remains admirable, within the scope of participatory research and egalitarianism the collaboration between the researchers and their Navajo participants is somewhat lacking. After all, the research agenda was set out about the researchers, and the analysis was carried out from the vantage point of the researchers' dominant White culture (see Mead, 1975). This critique and the subsequent increase in interest in reflexivity and positionality may well have also contributed to the turning point in relation to the use of photographs within social science research. Researchers not only realised but also externalised their concerns relating to their impact through the positioning of cameras, through what is being recorded and what is left out, as well as how photographs are arranged when they are shared (see Wolbert, 2000). Thus, gradually, in the spirit of coproduction in qualitative research, photographs re-entered the research space.

The new terminology in use at this time included 'image production' and 'photo elicitation'. Image production has undergone different phases of typologies and naming, but is essentially an approach whereby the research participants are asked to create or generate visual material for the purpose of the research (for example, Pauwels, 2020). Photo elicitation has also developed from the understanding that power hierarchies and dynamics in the researcher–participant relationship need to be addressed. However, the approach taken with photo elicitation is critiqued as less egalitarian because the images are used as a stimulus or provocation to aid and enhance interviewing (for example, Pauwels, 2015). Photo elicitation made its way into research relating to sports (for example, Curry, 1986; Snyder and Kane, 1990), and educational settings (Stockrocki, 1985), such as the study into the lived experience of women re-entering education after having been in care (Blinn and Harrist, 1991) in addition to ethnographic and anthropological studies in different rural communities (for example, Schwartz, 1989; Niessen, 1991).

From photo novella to photovoice

Eventually, in 1997, Wang and Burris coined the term 'photovoice' and made it popular, after having initially called the approach 'photo novella' (1994). Photovoice then was seen as an approach to carrying out research using photographs as a means to tell stories and to genuinely connect with audiences. The three key criteria that would distinguish photovoice from other research approaches using photographs were:

1. to enable people to record and reflect their community's strengths and concerns,
2. to promote critical dialogue and knowledge about important issues through large and small group discussion of photographs, and
3. to reach policymakers. (Wang and Burris, 1997, p 369)

Photovoice, thus, directly taps into Freire's (2017) problem-based education (see Chapter 2), feminist theory, and the efforts of activists, community educators, and photographers to enable and empower the marginalised. The scope for photovoice was seen to lie within the context of health and public health issues, especially with groups and communities who would otherwise be excluded from research and public debates relating to such topics. In their research Wang and Burris (1994, 1997) used photovoice with women in two rural Chinese counties. Their argument that photovoice enables, empowers, and includes as well as fosters action was made convincingly. By now, though, researchers across all disciplines use photographs as part of photovoice or photo elicitation studies. So let us therefore have a look at some of the benefits and drawbacks as outlined in more contemporary studies.

Strengths and weaknesses of photovoice

The benefits of photographic community data

In order to determine the strengths and weaknesses of photovoice, it may be best to return to its origins in the 1990s. The strengths highlighted by Wang and Burris (1994, 1997) themselves relate to the use of visuals or participatory approaches more generally as well as to the photovoice methodology specifically. One of their key arguments in favour of photovoice is the ability of photographs 'showing, rather than telling'. In short, photographs drive home inequalities or public shortcomings in ways that interview results or research reports would not be able to. Similarly, the authors argue that researchers' preconceptions and biases regarding the ability of rural participants could potentially lead to misconceptions and misunderstandings where research outcomes are concerned. By way of example, the researchers state how assuming participants' low level of education and lack of knowledge could be misinterpreted as the major challenge and obstacle to engagement in public life. In fact, the women participants very capably identified lack of basic provisions, such as water and transportation, as the most important factors for not being able to take part in public life. While these advantages are indeed important, they are not necessarily linked directly to the use of photovoice. We see here that even the researchers most widely associated with the development of photovoice as a research method conflate their approach with other aspects of research. What is recognised as a strength of photovoice in itself is the closeness to the participants' communities demonstrated because the photographs belong to and come from the members of these communities. For some researchers, this closeness to the community relates to concerns of authenticity and validity, which are often difficult concepts to engage with within qualitative research (Zurba et al, 2017). Other researchers emphasise the ease with which participants can be involved more directly, more immediately, and in a more empowering manner, in comparison with other participatory research approaches (Given et al, 2011; Mysyuk and Huisman, 2020; for a discussion of power dynamics and hierarchies, see Chapter 2). As a result, the predominant aspect of giving voice to individuals is the main driver of photovoice research (Evans-Agnew and Rosemberg, 2016).

The relative ease with which cameras can be managed and operated also means that commonly under-researched populations may be involved in research, such as older people (Novek et al, 2012), younger children (Shaw, 2021), international individuals whose first language is not the same as their community's first language (Wang and Hannes, 2014), and disabled communities (Anne, 2013). In addition, researchers feel that photovoice enables a level of triangulation of the data that could not be achieved with interviews on their own (Given et al, 2011). Finally, the argument of photography enabling individuals to delve deeper into their reflections, as outlined earlier (Harper, 2002), also is at play, because the photographs may trigger memory to enable the recall of experiences and therefore reach tacit knowledge (Van Auken et al, 2010). In turn, these advantageous aspects of photovoice enable researchers and communities to drive for social change as well as improve relationships within or between communities and stakeholders (Milne and Muir, 2020).

Practical and critical concerns

The most widely reported disadvantages of photovoice relate to time and resources. Many scholars outline how time-consuming photovoice is, when it is considered from the recruitment of the participants to training the participants for data generation and data analysis to then carrying out the data collection and analysis, as well as to look after the accurate processing, storing, and maintaining of photographs (for example, Pullman and Robson, 2006; Given et al, 2011; Sutton-Brown, 2014; Mysyuk and Huisman, 2020). In addition, many scholars also mention the cost involved in supplying cameras to their research participants for them to be able to take the pictures in their communities (for example, Wang and Burris, 1997; Meo, 2010; Sutton-Brown, 2014).

However, photovoice attracts more significant critique. Researchers commenting on the disadvantages or weaknesses of photovoice often highlight the issue of inclusivity. Photovoice by its definition is meant to be empowering, inclusive, yet, researchers feel there is a danger that some populations will be further excluded and marginalised, as they struggle to operate cameras and can therefore not be involved in such studies because it is difficult to adjust the approach for participants' potential specific needs (Mysyuk and Huisman, 2020). Sutton-Brown (2014) addresses this fallacy of inclusivity particularly well, when she highlights how researchers refer to wanting to include the vulnerable (Wang and Burris, 1997), the socially invisible (Wang et al, 1996), and the marginalised (Carlson et al, 2006). While she does not question the intentions of these and other scholars, she quite rightly challenges the notions of such terms. The mere fact that researchers use such labels highlights their 'superiority' over participants. Thus, these researchers do not actually minimise the power differential between them as researchers and participants, they only mask it somehow.

Analytically, photovoice also poses a challenge. Researchers disagree on whether the photographs should be seen as a complete data set and separate from any interview or conversation (Given et al, 2011). Yet, the interpretation of photographs requires skill sets that even they themselves struggle with although they are trained, quite unlike most research participants (Meo, 2010). These two arguments are further indicators of how photovoice masks some of the most important aspects in research. The original aim of the photovoice approach was to enable participation among communities who would otherwise potentially be left out. By then restricting the value of the photographs those individuals supply or by suggesting that the individuals' interpretations do not constitute full analysis, we run the risk of devaluing and undermining that very noble initial goal.

The missing pieces

I would like to conclude this brief outline of some of the strengths and weaknesses of photovoice with a caveat that is less well documented but a very significant aspect when determining the role and suitability of photovoice. As meta-analyses and systematic reviews of photovoice articles show (for example, Derr and Simons, 2020; Suprapto et al, 2020), there are only very few studies that truly reflect the spirit and definition as originally intended and outlined (Wang and Burris, 1997). This causes complexities and confusion, as it becomes more difficult to determine the actual impact the photovoice element of a research has if it is juxtaposed with and linked to narrative interviewing, for example. Once such research approaches are connected, researchers will find it difficult to know or to determine if the depth of their participants' reflections is due to the photovoice element or to the techniques of narrative interviewing.

Additionally, the complexities of research itself must not be disregarded. Within qualitative research, we generally recognise that society is in a state of flux and that developments often happen concurrently or messily rather than in a logical, linear fashion. Photovoice as an approach seems to gloss over this reality with its intention to be political and to ask for social change. Truth is, however, that photovoice sometimes instils a 'false sense of empowerment' (Wang et al, 1996, p 1397), and that in many instances the participants do not actually have the means to bring about the relevant change that photovoice advocates for and promises.

Photovoice in *Photovoice Reimagined*

As we have seen throughout this introductory chapter, photovoice is a powerful method of enquiry that seeks to privilege voices that are often under-represented. We have also seen that photovoice is not without its challenges or limitations. And that to an extent photovoice is not necessarily inherently different from other visual research approaches that include some participatory paradigm in their research design (Mitchell, 2011), especially if we accept that social change through photovoice is not a given. With the blurring of boundaries and adjustments made for specific research projects and target participants, the concepts, and terminologies of photovoice, photo elicitation, visual methods, and image production have become muddled further. Over time, projects using both approaches for one and the same study have increased significantly (for example, Oliffe and Bottorff, 2007; Kurtz and Wood, 2014; Kong et al, 2015; Minthorn and Marsh, 2016).

Disciplinary conventions and discipline-specific terminologies further compound the issue.

Many a sociological research, for example, relates to the use of visual methodologies and applies approaches using images (for example, Power, 2003; Harper, 2005), without calling the work 'photovoice' or 'photo elicitation'. As a consequence, there is no longer a purist distinction. My intention with this book is not to further confuse, nor to conflate the issues. Instead, I try to show that photo elicitation and photovoice along with other visual methods of enquiry sit on a continuum that ranges from minimal participant engagement with limited social change to maximum participation for active transformation among the participants, the researchers, their respective communities, and the stakeholders in wider society (see Figure 1.1).

In most likelihood, photovoice will be moved somewhere between the centre towards the right of the graph in Figure 1.1, whereas photo elicitation sits somewhere between the centre and the left of the graph. However, where on this continuum photovoice and photo elicitation, and, indeed, any other visual approaches are located definitively, depends on the circumstances of the individual research, the design of the project, as well as the paradigms and theoretical foundations a researcher subscribes to. For example, a number of scholars consider research methods using photography or other visual materials as a form of arts-based approach that aims to engage in social justice issues (Barone and Eisner, 2011; Leavy, 2020; see Chapter 2). Thus, a researcher using photo elicitation from the vantage point of arts-based research would probably be located further to the right on the graph (see Figure 1.1) than a scholar using photo elicitation as a technique to enhance interviewing. Bearing in mind the history of photovoice, along with the flexibility and fluidity outlined in these final sections, let me now turn to how to design photovoice research.

Figure 1.1: Continuum of participant engagement and social change

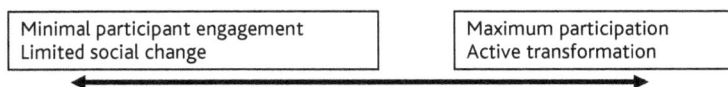

Minimal participant engagement Limited social change		Maximum participation Active transformation

End of chapter tasks

1. Having read about the history of photovoice, experiment with photography. Think about who you are as a researcher, and create a single photograph or a series of photographs to represent that experience. I recommend you journal about this experience in writing or by developing further creative responses.

2. Open a magazine or newspaper at a random page and look at the image(s) you can see. Consider how the image illustrates or exemplifies the adjacent text, and in how far the adjacent text is required to understand the image(s). In your journal, record your thoughts.

2

Designing photovoice research

Chapter aims

- To outline philosophical and theoretical foundations in photovoice research.

- To identify potential research foci and questions for photovoice research.

- To offer considerations relating to participants in photovoice research.

Introduction

As a reader of this book, you are, in all likelihood, considering to include photovoice to some extent and in some way in your research. However, before describing the process of data collection, analysis, and dissemination in Chapters 3, 4, and 5, it is important to consider the foundations of and for photovoice. As the brief outline in Chapter 1 has shown, photovoice in its purest sense is not merely a data collection method, but an entire philosophy founded on specific theoretical frameworks. Philosophical and theoretical principles, in turn, have a bearing on the entire research design as well as on its realisation in practice. Therefore, what may appear to be an interesting method of data collection or approach to analysis, may not actually be suitable for the kind of research you would like to undertake, for the type of research questions you are planning to ask, or for the demographic of research participants you would like to involve.

Of course, if we realise that a research approach is not perfect for our research question and/or context we can adjust that existing paradigm to better fit our purposes. Many researchers have done exactly that. I, for one, see no harm at all in that, as it shows that we engage with our research, that we understand the intricacies and complexities of the particular setting we work in, and that we attend to those, rather than gloss them over or ignore them.

Yet, I do worry about researchers making adjustments to existing paradigms light-heartedly. I think that the conflation of terminologies I discussed in Chapter 1 resulted, at least in parts, from adaptations that were made without having clarified the different stances and viewpoints at play. I am by no means a purist myself, and so I would not insist on others to be. Instead, I would like researchers to be able to make informed decisions and to justify their deliberate choices appropriately with the help of relevant literature. It is in this spirit that I am asking you to read what follows. In this chapter, I begin with a more detailed outline of the philosophical and theoretical foundations of photovoice before discussing the research foci and questions that photovoice studies may explore. The chapter concludes with a consideration of participants, as well as their recruitment and engagement in photovoice.

Philosophical and theoretical foundations

In Chapter 1, I mentioned that photovoice was developed by drawing on feminist theory, and on Freire's (2017, 2021) approach to empowerment and critical consciousness in education (Wang and Burris, 1994, 1997). I also briefly touched upon the consideration of photovoice as an arts-based approach (Barone and Eisner, 2011; Leavy, 2020), particularly in relation to social justice issues and the activist efforts of educators and photographers to bring about change (Wang and Burris, 1994, 1997; Barone and Eisner, 2011; Leavy, 2020). In the following, I provide a more detailed overview of these foundational principles and what they mean for photovoice research.

Photovoice according to Wang and Burris (1994, 1997)

Empowerment and critical consciousness

The starting point for photovoice is the educational foundation brought forward by Freire's pedagogies of the oppressed and education for critical consciousness (2017, 2021). In Freire's understanding, education was not meant to be the mere transfer of knowledge from teacher to student, but to empower and enable students to develop independent, critical thought. Learning, in his view, would be most effective when teacher and learner enter a dialogue, through which they can collaboratively work through the problems they are faced with. Further, Freire argues that this dialogic form of teaching and learning is only possible through an iterative process of reflecting on previous knowledge and experience, then acting upon those reflections, then, in turn, reflecting on the outcomes of these actions. Wang and Burris (1994, 1997) applied these principles by formally recognising the participants as experts and the researchers as facilitators, almost as learners in dialogue with the experts. Sense-making of data and experiences therefore is not an isolated act undertaken by the researcher in their office, but in collaboration with the participant-experts in a dialogic fashion.

Feminist theory

The second theoretical strand for Wang and Burris's (1994, 1997) development of photovoice is feminism. By focusing on women as a research topic as well as participants, the originators aimed at counteracting male bias in research. To this end, they draw on Reinharz's (1992) principles of feminist scholarship, and more specifically on Linton's (1990) characteristics of feminist research. According to Linton (1990, p 277), scholarship can classified as feminist only if:

1. women are the active central focus/subject;
2. cooperative group activity is the predominant modus operandi;
3. there is a recognized need for liberation from the oppression of the status quo;
4. issues affecting women are identified, and strategies for action are developed;

5. there is an open, inclusive, accessible, creative, dynamic process between people, among activities, or in relation to ideas; and
6. there is a commitment to respect and include women's ideas, theories, experiences, and action strategies from diverse experiences that appear to be, and sometimes are, in conflict.

In their own work, Wang and Burris (1994, 1997) observed these features closely, although in their writing they merely advocated for rather than demanded more conscious decisions for including women as research foci or subjects. What shines through from these characteristics is the emphasis on cooperation and inclusiveness for the benefit of bringing about change and transformation in order to subvert oppressive conditions.

Documentary photography

Wang and Burris (1994, 1997) name documentary photography as their third foundational principle for photovoice. For the originators documentary photography was not without its faults. Drawing on Rosler (1989) they critiqued intensively the practice of photographing for dreadful 'combinations of exoticism, tourism, voyeurism, psychologism and metaphysics, trophy hunting – careerism' (p 306). For Wang and Burris (1994, 1997), the only way to combat this voyeurism was to hand cameras over to members of the respective communities under research rather than asking a relative outsider to take photographs. In this regard, their work directly links to Worth and Adair's (1972) *Through Navajo Eyes* and other researchers who had also experimented with upending the conventions of documentary photography in the late 1980s and early 1990s. Most notably, three researchers worked with what would have been considered vulnerable, marginalised populations, such as children in the Appalachians (Ewald, 1985), children who experienced homelessness (Hubbard, 1991), and peasants and workers (Spence, 1995), and asked them to capture their experiences using a camera. By asking community members to step up as community photographers, Wang and Burris (1994, 1997) actively sought to disrupt the conventional power dynamics between researchers, participants, and stakeholders, while also looking to refute objectification of communities.

Connecting the three strands

What permeates through these three foundational strands is the active rejection of existing power dynamics by introducing inclusive, egalitarian, participatory measures into the research process. Photovoice in this context truly is an entire philosophy. The paradigm requires researchers to engage with their own positionality in a critical-reflexive manner in order to overcome the challenges posed by their standing in society vis-a-vis their participants. The researchers' role is then to subvert typical hierarchies and to place themselves such that they recognise their insignificance when it comes to the experience their participant-experts relay.

Although these are admirable aims, the practice of photovoice research is often somewhat different. For example, a systematic review of 19 articles reporting on photovoice research with women as research participants found significant tensions between the researchers' aims with their study and the target to empower participants through photovoice (Coemans et al, 2019). A different scoping analysis considered 32 articles using photovoice within the contexts of sustainability education, environment, and conservation (Derr and Simons, 2020). The aim of this analysis was to identify to what extent photovoice research carried out in the 2000s continued to apply the emancipatory intents of the method. While many of the studies under review considered the purpose of photovoice research in its transformative nature, findings show that the emancipatory effects of photovoice are most often not met. The authors therefore specifically recommend researchers considering photovoice to focus on change more proactively by employing the method consistently and by adding evaluative elements that could clearly ascertain the effectiveness of the approach (Derr and Simons, 2020).

Truth is, however, that researchers often find themselves navigating particular criteria in order to publish an article. There are expectations relating to the length of a publication, the content, and design or layout. Authors may therefore find they are not able to focus on a specific aspect of their work, be that theoretical frameworks, philosophical outlooks, sample size, argument, and the like, as they may prove contentious or incompatible with the academic journal they are targeting. As researchers we work within much wider constraints from employers, grant funders, examination standards, societal expectations, and within these constraints we may not be able to achieve the ideal of feminist empowerment and transformation that photovoice demands.

Expanding the theoretical toolkit

In the previous section I highlighted that (1) systematic reviews raise concerns about researchers not fully complying with the criteria of photovoice, that (2) Wang and Burris (1994, 1997) themselves assert that the predominant function of photovoice is to remove oppression, of which the oppression of women is only one form, and that (3) researchers face a multitude of constraints regarding their work. Given that there are these issues surrounding the application of the purest form of photovoice, we may do well to expand our theoretical toolkit to be able to adjust the method and to justify the choices we make. Figure 1.1 demonstrated the continuum of participant engagement and social change, and in order to find our personal position on this continuum we should consider cognate frameworks.

(Feminist) participatory action research

In the late 1980s, participatory research approaches that had first been developed earlier started gaining traction. The philosophical starting point for participatory research is the recognition that the dominant knowledge generation in research often favours the pursuit of objective truths, rather than accepting reality as subjective interpretation and representation. Participatory research, by contrast, aimed at

1. valuing people's knowledge, thus recognising participants as experts,
2. refining capacities, thus enabling participants to conduct research themselves,
3. enabling members of the general public to appropriate the knowledge of the dominant system,

4. focussing on people's perspective rather than the researchers' views, and
5. liberating the minds of the poor and the oppressed. (Tandon, 1988, pp 10–11)

Within the scope of these aims Tandon (1988, p 13) stipulated three key criteria determining participatory research:

1. people's role in setting the agenda of the inquiry;
2. people's participation in data collection and analysis; and
3. people's control over the use of outcome and the whole process.

Participatory action research is another cognate to participatory research, which is most commonly attributed to the social psychologist Kurt Lewin (1946). Lewin (1946) argued for research with impact and meaning for the researchers and the communities they study. His action research framework demands close collaboration between researchers and the researched communities, but also outlines the need for planning for effective, meaningful, and lasting change in order to ensure marginalised communities are able to overcome the challenges they face. Participatory action research, therefore, connects Tandon's (1988) participatory framework with Lewin's (1946) action research.

This combined set of criteria for participatory action research is not vastly divergent from Linton's (1990) six characteristics for feminist research. In fact, commentators at the time remarked on how the two frameworks seek to achieve the same goals of doing research for social justice purposes but are 'unconnected approaches, largely ignorant of each other' (Maguire, 1987, p 81). Maguire (1987) took it upon herself to rectify that by developing a stance towards a feminist participatory action research. One reason for the initial separation, but also the difficulty in retracing the steps between participatory action research and feminist participatory action research, will have been the interpretation of feminism and feminist theory. Although there is the connecting theme of rejecting and disrupting oppression across all forms of feminism(s), there is actually

no one, unifying feminist theory; neither does there exist a consensus on how diverse feminist theoretical contributions should be categorized. (Brisolara, 2014, p 4)

Yet, in Brisolara's (2014) view, all feminist theories are connected by the thread of recognising positionality and standpoint within society. It is that acknowledgement that enables us to also ascertain our relative position of power within society more broadly, and vis-a-vis our participants, more specifically. The relationship between feminist participatory action research and photovoice lies with the focus on the standpoint and positioning of participants. Both frameworks consider the participants as central and at the heart of all considerations. Simultaneously, both frameworks ask for maximum participation for the purpose of effecting social change and transformation. Latz and Mulvihill (2017) explicitly argue that photovoice is in effect 'a form of participatory action research' (p 39) because the main emphasis is the desire to bring about change. Although the inclusion of feminist theory may feel somewhat deterring for some, they argue that researchers should not shy away from embracing the basic 'tenets of feminist epistemology and methodology' (Latz and Mulvihill, 2017, p 38). For them, feminist theory counters an outlook on the world that marginalises women in a patriarchal society, and they contend that there are many marginalised subgroups in patriarchally structured cultures.

Creative research methods and arts-based research

In the contemporary social sciences research landscape, creative research methods and arts-based research have gained significant popularity. Although, as ever, the individual designs and philosophies differ, many basic tenets apply to a majority of schools of thought. The prevailing foundational principle for creative research methods and arts-based research is the fact that human beings draw on a variety of representations to express themselves, and that each of these forms of representations has its own merits and challenges (Barone and Eisner, 2011). From this follows that researchers can and indeed should not attempt to collect data in a uniform way of interviews or surveys, but should instead open up communication and expression to include arts-based and creative means. In turn, the outcomes of such creative and/or arts-based forms of expression contribute to human understanding, as they are experienced as enlightening and illuminating (Leavy, 2020).

Naturally, not all creative methods fall within the realm of arts-based research, and equally, not all forms of arts-based research relate to photovoice research. There are nonetheless significant overlaps. Many forms of creative methods and arts-based research seek to redress the power hierarchy between the dominant and minoritised populations of a society. In addition, arts-based research, in particular, considers and indeed values the impact of the creative output on its audience. Through encouraging aestheticism and verisimilitude, arts-based research seeks to connect with its audience in order to emotionally engage and foster a turn to action (Leavy, 2015, 2020). The connection to photovoice seems evident. In fact, many handbooks include photovoice as an example of a creative and/or arts-based research method (for example, Knowles and Cole, 2008; Kara, 2015, 2020; Cahnmann-Taylor and Siegesmund, 2018; Leavy, 2018). This umbrella function of the terms is also a factor contributing to the confusion around photovoice, as the philosophical and theoretical foundations are probably not as well explored within such generic handbooks as they could be. The aesthetic quality, the general applicability of the representation, and the implicit call for action are all aspects of creative and/or arts-based research that apply equally well to photovoice, and so it is not surprising that the boundaries are crossed rather than delineated. Photovoice and arts-based research differs most significantly where participants' reflections are concerned. Participants' reflections, thus the researcher's efforts to collaborate with participants, to make sense of photographs, and to determine their relevance for wider societal matters, are a key element in photovoice research. In arts-based research, participants' reflections are most often not afforded the same attention.

Embodied Inquiry

Photovoice and other visual research methods also feature heavily within the contexts of Embodied Inquiry. Embodied Inquiry is not a paradigm per se, but an approach to research that centralises the body, that of the participant, as well as of the researcher (Leigh and Brown, 2021). The philosophical foundations for Embodied Inquiry are phenomenology (our being-in-the-world), hermeneutics (the interpretative nature of our reality), three cornerstones of human understanding and communication (that human understanding is embodied, that language is insufficient and inexact, and that communication and human understanding are metaphorical), and multimodality (that different forms of meaning-making and expression are inextricably linked) (Leigh and Brown, 2021, pp 26–31). As a consequence of these foundational principles, Embodied Inquiry specifically asks for means of expressions that go beyond conventional interviewing or surveying techniques and that often draw on arts-based and creative methods. In this context, the use of photographs in some forms of photo elicitation appears to be an obvious and indeed preferred choice.

Instead of emphasising the transformative nature of research, however, Embodied Inquiry focuses on the participatory connection to support participants in their attempt to make sense of bodily and embodied experiences that may sometimes be difficult to explore and explain. It does that by asking participants to supply photographs that express and represent those experiences. As such, photovoice is again delineated as a means to achieving the end of expression and communication, like in creative and arts-based research. Yet, unlike in arts-based research, the participants' reflections relating to their embodiment and its representations play a pivotal role within Embodied Inquiry.

Connecting photovoice, its foundations, and the continuum

The overview of philosophical and theoretical principles underpinning photovoice exemplifies where some of the confusion around photovoice and photo elicitation originates: depending on the researcher's beliefs and assumptions, photovoice is either a fixed paradigm and fully developed framework that must be applied as is; or photovoice is a method of data collection within a much broader participatory and emancipatory framework that can be applied more loosely.

It may be helpful at this stage to revisit Figure 1.1 that outlined the continuum of participation and social change.

Figure 2.1 should help identify some of the differences between the theoretical foundations outlined in this chapter.

As Figure 2.1 demonstrates, photovoice as originally developed and advocated for (Wang and Burris, 1994, 1997) emphasises the maximum participation and active transformation on the far right of the continuum, while documentary photography in its original interpretation that was so starkly critiqued sits at the left extreme of the continuum. Participatory action research and feminist participatory action research are roughly at the same position on the continuum, with their main difference lying in the research focus either being more narrowly focused on feminist issues or not. In terms of participation and transformation, however, photovoice as a method within (feminist) participatory action research is still very closely related to the original intentions of the framework. Photovoice as sitting under the umbrella of creative research methods and Embodied Inquiry, for example, is situated much further to the centre of the continuum. This is because although they focus on participation there is a definitive lack of emphasis on transformation and social change within creative research methods and Embodied Inquiry. Feminist theory, by contrast, asks for social change for the benefit of women, but probably does not engage women as participants to the same extent that participatory approaches do, for example. For the sake of completeness, I have added the term photo elicitation to signify photovoice as a method. Of course, any schematisation can only be a simplification because the actual positioning of theories on a continuum depends on the full design and process of the research. Yet, the graph helps illustrate further why the terms photovoice and photo elicitation are often used interchangeably, and why some projects claiming to be photovoice studies may actually not be.

Photovoice research foci and questions

So far, I have already referenced many articles relating to photovoice and photo elicitation, which demonstrate a wide array of research foci and research questions. Photovoice has been used in education and higher education, sports, health, environment and conservation, information science, land management, food

Figure 2.1: Continuum of participant engagement and social change in photovoice

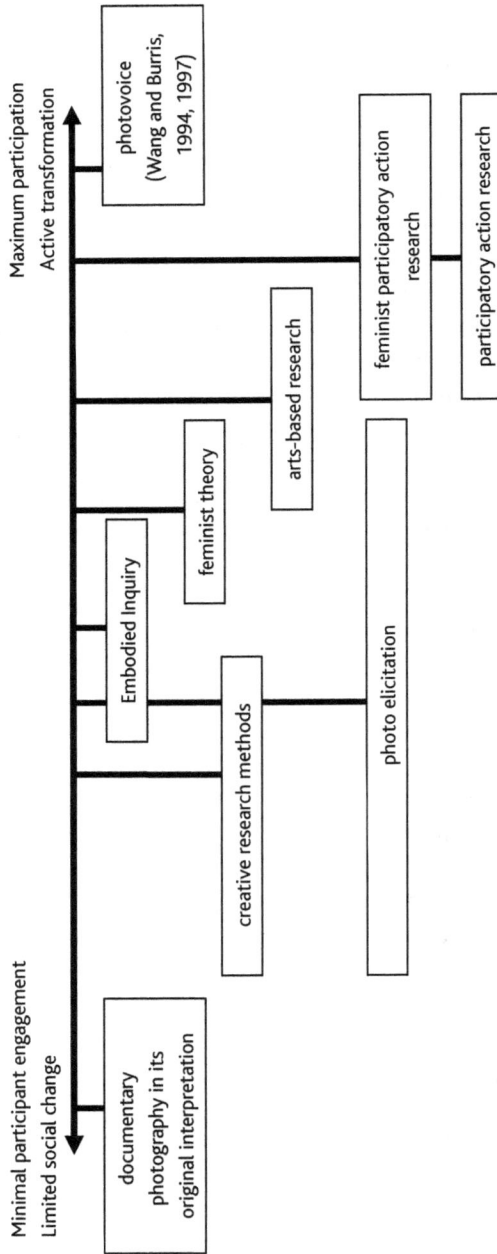

geography, sense of belonging and identity, cultural studies, and the hospitality industry. Although photovoice draws on feminist theory it is by no means limited to feminist studies or female participants only. In short, there do not seem to be any disciplinary limitations to where photovoice is applied. The geographical spread of photovoice articles is similarly vast with articles reporting on studies carried out in China, Belgium, Africa, Sumatra, and among the Indigenous cultures of North America to name just a few. With Google Scholar offering 12,600 articles relating to photovoice that were published between 2020 and 2022, there literally is no restriction in using photovoice. Not all photovoice studies may be of the best possible standard, just like the publication of any qualitative research article is variable in quality. What it ultimately comes down to is the researcher's understanding and application of philosophical tenets and the suitability of photovoice in addressing the research question. With that, let us consider the kinds of research questions that photovoice answers.

Again, we have to bear in mind that photovoice may either take the form of a purist stance aimed at social change, or the potentially less transformative positioning of Embodied Inquiry or creative research methods where the photovoice element focuses merely on engaging participants differently. The question a researcher poses will depend on where on the continuum they want to position themselves and their work. Many scholars reporting on photovoice projects highlight the importance of photovoice in uncovering their participants' lived experience and perceptions (for example, Novek et al, 2012; Plunkett et al, 2013). For example, Novek et al (2012) asked their participants, who were older adults, to capture the age-friendliness of their communities. Then, in subsequent group discussions, the participants collaborated to develop strategies and recommendations to improve their communities' age-friendliness. In a different study (Lindhout et al, 2021) the researchers recruited workers in a factory, nurses in a hospital department, and ironworkers on a construction site to explore how they experience health and safety and safety management in their respective workplaces. Because the community members themselves take the photographs there is a potential to collectively identify best practices, as well as to jointly consider suggestions for improvement. Photovoice has also been used effectively within the scope of mental health issues with some researchers exploring the effectiveness of an intervention (for example, Cabassa et al, 2013a, 2013b), whereas others focused on the lived experience of the mental health illness itself (for example, Clements, 2012; Panazzola and Leipert, 2013) or sought to understand health behaviours and patients' commitment to find support (Rosen et al, 2011).

In all these studies, the transformative nature of photovoice was foregrounded. As a result, the questions relating to lived experience and perceptions were viewed from a more evaluative, evaluating, and directive position. By contrast, studies that use photovoice as a research method in order to enhance interviews may also ask questions about lived experience and perceptions, but will do so with less determination to uncover shortcomings or gaps.

The example relating to older adults and the age-friendliness of their communities (Novek et al, 2012) could have been framed differently in that it could have asked the question along the lines of 'What does it feel like to be old in your community?' In effect, the research focus remains the same, but the framing of the research question is somewhat different. Instead of asking participants to capture the age-friendliness in their communities, thereby effectively directing them what to do, the research question here is more of an open-ended question about experiences and perceptions. Within the scope of a research proposal the authors may well have formulated a question. But the design of the photovoice research is such that the photovoice element becomes a task or directive along the lines of 'Capture ... and then let us identify ways to ...'. In research that uses photovoice as a method of data collection the research is more clearly linked to a formal research question. And the questions that researchers pose are then along the lines of 'What is the participants' lived experience of ...?', 'How do participants make sense of ...?', or 'What does it feel like to ...?'

To further illustrate this difference, I now draw upon two examples that have been formally defined as photo elicitation studies rather than photovoice research. Within tourism and management, research explored tourists' experiences in Andalusia, Spain, using photographs (Matteucci, 2013). Drawing on previous studies using visual methods, and specifically on Harper (2002), the researcher purposefully selected images related to flamenco-dancing that were then shown to the participants during the research interview as a means to stimulate conversation, to elicit further responses, and to triangulate what the participants had said before. The research question for this project was

> how [do] tourists experience intangible heritage, in the form of flamenco music and dance courses. (Matteucci, 2013, p 191)

Similarly, in their study Hatten et al (2013) focused on the use of photo elicitation as an approach to collecting data. The researchers were interested in how individuals make sense of their personal and professional identity in the context of cross-disciplinary engagements. The participants were asked to bring photographs to interviews with the researchers offering prompts, such as

> Please find 4 pictures (although you may use as many as 6):
>   One that represents something about you as a person.
>   One that represents something about you as a professional.
>   One that represents your (primary) discipline.
>   One that represents your cross-disciplinary work.
> (Hatten et al, 2013, p 23898)

Although this study required the participants to generate images and to make sense of those images in subsequent interviews, it does not have that emphasis on the transformative nature of photovoice research. This is then also reflected in the research question, which was formulated as

> [what are] participants' experiences with cross-disciplinary work and their evolving understanding of cross-disciplinarity, how [does] this relate to their understanding of engineering, their 'home' discipline, and their sense of self within and across these spaces? (Hatten et al, 2013, p 23897)

As mentioned before, due to confusion over terminologies, publishing expectations, and criteria, as well as misconceptions relating to philosophical and theoretical frameworks, many photo elicitation studies are presented under the umbrella of photovoice. Ultimately, it is the formulation of the research question in relation to the nature of the research that helps us identify the difference and determine what constitutes photovoice. If the research question is open-ended, the project is less likely to be a photovoice research than if the research is formulated as a command or directive along the lines of 'Show me ...' or 'Capture ...'.

Participants in photovoice research

Just as the research foci of the photovoice studies I mentioned so far are varied, the participant demographic is, too. As the overarching aim of photovoice research is to centralise marginalised populations, participants in photovoice research are women (for example, Bunster, 1977; Wang and Burris, 1994, 1997; Wang et al, 1996; Panazzola and Leipert, 2013), older adults (for example, Rosen et al, 2011; Novek et al, 2012; Mysuyk and Huisman, 2020), young children (for example, Ewald, 1985; Hubbard, 1991; Shaw, 2021), secondary school pupils (Mental Health Literacy and Diversity, nd), international students (for example, Wang and Hannes, 2014), patients with physical and mental health issues (for example, Wang and Burris, 1994, 1997; Oliffe and Bottorff, 2007; Clements, 2012; Cabassa et al, 2013a, 2013b; Panazzola and Leipert, 2013), or injured sportspeople (for example, Curry, 1986; Snyder and Kane, 1990). In short, participants generally are populations that are considered as marginalised (Carlson et al, 2006), vulnerable (Wang and Burris, 1997), and/or socially invisible (Wang et al, 1996), and so they should be in order for photovoice to be effective in its transformative nature. However, classifications are inherently problematic (Sutton-Brown, 2014), and so, the question arises who decides on what makes a participant marginalised, vulnerable, and/or socially invisible, and how privileged must that person be to be able to take such a decision.

From this the question arises, how as researchers we should approach the recruitment of participants for photovoice projects.

In practice, participant recruitment for photovoice studies does not differ too greatly from the general opportunities afforded in qualitative research. Typical recruitment strategies tend to include the use of social media and snowballing, along with direct mailing and the contact through mailing lists, with some researchers offering incentives, while others do not have sufficient funding to offer payment and therefore rely on the prospective participants' goodwill. Articles also report on researchers' concern around hard-to-reach groups of participants, participants in rural or less accessible areas, participants from different demographical and socio-economic status, and participants with protected characteristics, such as race, ethnicity, gender, sexuality, disability, and the intersectional experiences of those (see Newington and Metcalfe, 2014; van Wijk, 2014; Friedman et al, 2015; Sikkens et al, 2017; Abrams et al, 2020) with Bonisteel et al (2021) offering a particularly comprehensive publication on participant recruitment. However, we need to remind ourselves that many studies employing photovoice are in effect not photovoice projects according to Wang and Burris (1994, 1997). When it comes to using photovoice with maximum participation and active transformation in mind, then the participant recruitment strategy may need to be somehow different. After all, for photovoice to function in that form the research need comes from the participants in the first instance. As a result, the participant group is most likely an already established group of individuals. If, however, the participants shall form a new group, then recruitment will be purposeful according to specific inclusion criteria, such as 'gender, ethnicity, disability, or health status' (Sutton-Brown, 2014, p 172; see also Wang, 1999). At this stage, it may be helpful for researchers to reach out to gatekeepers and insiders to the participant group, if they themselves may not have immediate access to the required communities to form a group of seven to ten participants.

Unfortunately, being a participant in a photovoice study is not necessarily easy or meaningful. While photovoice does offer the unique opportunity to community members to be involved in exploring their lived experiences and identifying recommendations to improve their status quo, there are systems and structures that may impede meaningful engagement and actual transformation. For example, for their study Warne et al (2013) recruited students as participants who were young adults aged between 16 and 20. The research focus was to explore students' perceptions on what makes them feel and work well in their school with a view to identify gaps to be redressed collectively. Although the research was managed and carried out successfully, the researchers identified significant impediments to the young adults' participation and engagement in photovoice. These challenges arose from existing structures and processes within the school context, where the research was set. Teachers were too used to being experts that they felt unable to hand over the responsibility for the photovoice project to their students.

In effect, the system of oppression that photovoice openly critiques is so ingrained and entrenched that, even with the express purpose of subverting it, the participants cannot escape it. The answer to this conundrum lies in the researcher's role. In photovoice that role is determined as a facilitator with the participants being described as experts. Facilitator is a useful term here, as it allows us to think of the researcher as someone who empowers the participants as experts, but who also enables the research itself by ensuring the structural parameters are appropriate. When we embark on photovoice research we may not necessarily be aware of nor expect the potential limitations such as those described in the Swedish study of students (Warne et al, 2013). Yet, as researchers it is our responsibility to manage our participants' expectations and to do what we can to ensure their wellbeing. The recruitment of participants, therefore, comes with our responsibility to not further marginalise, but also to not overstate what the research project can achieve, so as to not disappoint our participants in the long run.

In their article about participatory research, James and Shaw (2022) refer to a form of choreography where the researcher navigates their position within the research between 'stepping in', 'stepping out', and 'stepping on toes'. Although not specifically relating to photovoice, the authors highlight the tensions between remaining in charge of the research in order to ensure the research remains on point and participants are not harmed (stepping on toes), handing over responsibility and control to the participants (stepping out), and supporting the participants with their research, especially where they may be missing some expertise or skill (stepping in). The handing over and maintaining of control over the research is also the topic of a systematic review that specifically explored whose voice is it that is reported and disseminated from photovoice research (Evans-Agnew and Rosemberg, 2016). The findings show that participant voice is most often present in the areas that are ultimately hidden from public view. Thus, researchers emphasise the role of participants during data collection and sense-making, but when it comes to publications and reports participants' images are often not shared, nor are participants involved in the process of writing up the project. It is that difference between the potential of photovoice for enhancing minoritised voices and its actual application of glossing over or hiding these voices that is so widely critiqued in photovoice.

Once researchers recruit photovoice participants by the exclusion criteria of how vulnerable or marginalised or socially invisible they are, they have a duty to ensure they are not further othering them, but instead amplify their voices in and for society. We will return to some of these aspects throughout the next chapters, where I will focus on data collection, analysis, and dissemination, as well as ethical, methodological, and practical considerations.

End of chapter tasks

1. Reflect on your philosophical outlooks and your theoretical frameworks. Explore how you may be able to reconcile those with the use of photography in research and where on the continuum (see Figure 2.1) you would see yourself operating. Use your journal to record your reflections and thoughts.

2. Consider a research focus and develop the corresponding research question. Try to formulate that as a true question for a project using photovoice as a method for data collection and as a command and call for action for a true photovoice research. Journal about your research question.

3

Photovoice in and as data collection

Chapter aims

- To position photovoice as a method and as a framework.

- To identify the different forms of photovoice data collection.

- To offer guidance and practical steps for photovoice in data collection.

Introduction

In Chapters 1 and 2, I outlined the continuum of participant engagement and social action, and how photovoice may function as a data collection method, as well as a research paradigm. This positioning on the continuum not only has a bearing on the design of a photovoice project, but also on its practical application. Probably, the most significant impact of the philosophical outlook on photovoice lies with how data is viewed, which, in turn, shapes how data collection takes place.

As I have shown in Chapters 1 and 2, research that is undertaken under the umbrella term of photovoice would fit into the categories of photo elicitation and photovoice. One the one hand, photovoice continues in its original intention as a framework with a clear philosophical stance for carrying out research; on the other hand, photovoice nowadays includes, extends to, and overlaps with photo elicitation. This is where photovoice has become a method for data collection. In Figure 2.1, I introduced the different views of photovoice in connection to related philosophical and theoretical frameworks. What is perhaps less obvious from that graph is how researchers view photovoice along that continuum. Figure 3.1 seeks to illustrate more clearly the continuum of photovoice.

The main principles of photovoice remain the role of participant engagement and social change. Depending on the detailed design of a photovoice study social change or transformation and participant engagement are on a sliding scale somewhere between 'some' and 'maximum', with photovoice as a framework is very clearly situated on the maximum extreme. I deliberately reframe photo elicitation to photovoice as a method, based on my experience as research methods teacher. Some may dislike my approach here, as it is seen to add to the confusion between photo elicitation and photovoice. In my experience, however, a continuum from minimal to maximum participation and limited social change to active transformation is understood more easily and readily, than two separate approaches that overlap but are philosophically different to one another. We have seen that in practice the boundaries between photovoice and photo elicitation are so blurred that it is often difficult to untangle the philosophical and methodological outlooks in academic publications. The current funding environment in higher education represents a significant impetus for this development: the egalitarian, participatory philosophy in photovoice as framework projects is not practically realisable when academics and scholars apply for funding with *their* research questions and visions for research, rather than getting participants to frame the projects.

Having clarified the distinction between photovoice as a method and photovoice as a framework, let us now turn to

Figure 3.1: Photovoice reimagined

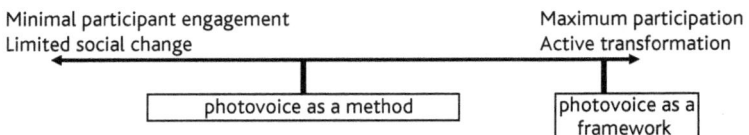

Minimal participant engagement   Maximum participation
Limited social change   Active transformation

photovoice as a method

photovoice as a framework

how the interpretation of photovoice impacts on data. Where photovoice is seen as a method, what constitutes data is not the photograph per se. Instead, the data remains the interview and sense-making around the photographs, with the photographs merely being an opportunity to make the interview conversation more engaging and to stimulate deeper reflections among the participants. Photovoice as a framework, by contrast, recognises the photographs as a valuable set of rich data in themselves. The conversations around and with the photographs are then group discussions among the participants with the researcher listening in and facilitating the discussion. Data, therefore, is the combination of the photographs and group discussions. The main differences between photovoice as a method and photovoice as a framework then lie with the positioning of researchers and participants in relation to the data, as well as the kind of sense-making that ensues from or in connection with the photographs. As sense-making really is an analytical process, I will turn to that in Chapter 4, where I discuss photovoice in and as data analysis. In this chapter, I focus entirely on the what and how of data collection.

Approaches to photovoice data collection

With photovoice taking such diverse forms, discussing data collection systematically becomes a somewhat complex undertaking. For the purpose of this book, I therefore propose three broader categories, within which I will explore different approaches to data collection: (1) photovoice as a method where researchers supply photographs for interviews, (2) photovoice as a method with participants bringing found or created photographs to interviews, and (3) photovoice as a framework. I use examples from literature and my own work to offer insight into each of these approaches, guidance on how to implement them, and a critical-reflective commentary on potential advantages and drawbacks.

Photovoice as method with researcher-supplied photographs

This approach recognises that human understanding and communication take more forms than the consciously verbal form and so draws on the thought that images being used in interviews will enhance the conversation. Rather than emphasising verbal communication, the use of images enables participants to draw on different parts of their consciousness that engages when they look at a photograph. The role of photographs in opening up insights into participants' experiences is well documented in anthropological literature, where it is referred to as the 'can-opener' effect or the 'golden key' moment (Collier and Collier, 1986, p 25). Effectively, this method is based on 'the simple idea of inserting a photograph into a research interview' (Harper, 2002, p 13) with the researcher supplying and bringing the photograph to that interview. Although this does indeed sound like a simple idea, there are not many studies describing the use of researcher-supplied images. The study of tourist experiences in Andalusia (Matteucci, 2013) is a notable exception. Within tourism research, the use of researcher-found photographs as data set is very common, but this is largely without the insertion of the photographs into interviews (Feighey, 2003). In other disciplines, such as education and sociology, researcher-found or -generated photographs within interviews are commonly recommended in theory-driven research. In such contexts, the researcher inserts carefully selected photographs into the interview to explore how participants understand or make sense of a particular issue, theory, or concept. This is best exemplified in the study of transition from non-formal primary to formal high schools in Bangladesh (Mahruf et al, 2007). The researchers' starting point was the idea that children's transition from non-formal primary to formal high schools would be impacted by external factors and the societal setting they find themselves in. The team drew on a particular framework describing society as an ecological system of factors at micro- (personal, individual), meso- (school, home, family, religion), and macro-level (culture, society, community). Photographs were then used in one phase of the study to specifically explore the usefulness of this theory of micro-, meso-, macro-levels in relation to understanding children's experiences. Similarly, Allen (2020, p 251) mentions that in her work she has introduced images to university students to investigate the theory that schools are sites for social (re)production. Understanding this use of photographs to test a particular theory (Allen, 2020), framework (Mahruf et al, 2007), or hypothesis (Matteucci, 2013) already points towards how this approach may be implemented in practice.

Implementing the method

For researcher-supplied photographs to be used effectively and meaningfully, the starting point is a clear vision of a theory, framework, or hypothesis that is to be evaluated. Rather than exploring participants' perceptions of and feelings about their lived experiences directly, there is a slight shift. The researcher here is not open to participants' own narratives, but is specifically trying to uncover the validity or appropriateness of a pre-formulated opinion. As a first step, therefore, the theory or framework need to be selected or developed carefully in order to provide the basis for this approach to data collection. Once that has been identified, the researcher needs to identify relevant and appropriate images with the choice between using found photographs and creating or generating specific photographs. The next step then is to decide which of the found or created images to use, how many of them to provide to participants, and how to introduce them within a research interview.

Unfortunately, the process of how researchers select and use the photographs they ultimately use in their interviews is rarely described in detail. For example, Matteucci (2013) mentions the use of image search engines on the internet, as well as directly perusing the websites of flamenco schools to gather the final selection of 18 images that were grouped into seven different categories. In their exploration of motivations for individuals to become voluntary tutors, Hurworth et al (2005) hint at a process of selecting and reviewing photographs that had been taken by the course leaders, who were neither the researchers, nor research participants. In their report on tourists' understanding of heritage sites in Hawke's Bay in New Zealand, Willson and McIntosh (2010) merely state that 44 images taken by the principal researcher were selected as interview prompts. Although there are some examples of photographs printed in the publication, it is not entirely clear which decisions were taken to photograph heritage sites and which views may have been left out. Similarly, the insertion into the interview is somehow glossed over. The researchers describe that showing too many images to participants may be overwhelming, but they do not clarify how many of the 44 images were actually shown. For anyone planning a project with researcher-supplied photographs, these examples are probably frustrating. However, if not explicitly enough, these studies do show some of the thought processes going into the selection or generation of photographs and just how complex the idea of 'inserting a photograph into a research interview' (Harper, 2002, p 13) really is. This in itself is an indication of the potential drawbacks of the approach.

Advantages and drawbacks of the method

Although I myself use images I bring to conversations, I do not tend to do that for research work and so have not published studies using researcher-supplied photographs. When I use researcher-supplied images, it tends to be in teaching settings as a stimulus for debates around the use of photographs in interviews and to exemplify the differences in conversations with and without photographs. Scholars refer to the depths of participants' reflections as a significant benefit and their reason for using photographs (for example, Hurworth et al, 2005; Carter and Ford, 2013; Allen, 2020). This is an argument I do not like to make, as I cannot be sure about the depths of reflections and richness of data being more or less, better or worse. We would have to test this hypothesis, which is obviously impossible. The argument I make is that the use of photography results in *different* data, and that makes it interesting for me as a pedagogical tool in research methods sessions. The advantages for providing photographs as a researcher, or in my case as an educationalist, relate to the selection of the photographs. I can make sure that the photographs are not distressing, that they do not display non-consenting individuals, and that I may be able to use the photographs in publications. Of course, the actual use of photographs will depend on whether I have sourced photographs from the internet, or if I have created them myself.

The reasons why I shy away from using researcher-supplied images in research contexts are linked to what I see as disadvantages of the method.

Above all, I am not confident about the selection of photographs. I always feel that I cannot possibly know which photographs are good or good enough to exemplify a particular concept or theory. We all interpret images differently, and come to them with all our previous experiences and knowledge. I would worry that I ended up choosing a photograph that would insert into the research interview a bias or prejudice based upon my ambiguous selection. That fear is not unfounded, as the images I bring to my research methods teaching sessions show. For these sessions, I use my family's postcard collections, as I can share these images without any worries around copyright issues and also in the knowledge that the postcards are not of a contentious nature or depicting sensitive topics. Yet, it is exactly this perceived blandness that makes it often difficult for workshop delegates to respond to and connect with the images that are there. By default, what the images depict and how they are interpreted is also more nondescript than emotionally charged. It still works as a teaching tool, as what people's experiences are does not fully matter. The lesson is about the advantages and drawbacks of using photographs. However, in a research interview participants' perceptions, opinions, feelings, and experiences do matter. And the insertion of inertia, indifference, or blandness, as would be the case with my postcards, would seriously impact the data.

Having said that, I recognise the benefits of researcher-found or -generated photographs: the theory-driven approach and the sameness of stimuli. When we plan a research project, we tend to have a particular theory, hypothesis, or framework in mind. Qualitative research handbooks warn against letting these preconceived ideas slip into our research interviews and advise us to remain open-minded to see the new with a fresh pair of eyes. In some research approaches bracketing (Husserl, 1960) and bridling (Dahlberg et al, 2011) are recommended strategies to counteract the gradual seeping in of previous knowledge. Yet, what if we did not ignore our previous knowledge, but instead, built on it? Photovoice as a method with researcher-supplied images would be a great way to do that. Admittedly, the difficulties around the selection of photographs remain. But once the photographs are chosen, they offer exciting opportunities to engage with research participants to further our own understanding. The fact that the photographs are then the same for all interviews is clearly another advantage, as the data set remains somewhat neat and manageable.

Photovoice as method with participant-supplied photographs

The approach of photovoice as method with participant-supplied photographs sits a little bit further to the right of the continuum by comparison with photovoice as method with researcher-supplied photographs (see Figure 3.1). Across publications of articles the data collection through photovoice as a method using participant-supplied photographs is probably the most common. For example, the approach has been used in research exploring palliative care nurses' experiences when caring for patients at the end of life (Alvariza et al, 2020), for the exploration of knowledge production in the context of higher education (Kortegast et al, 2019), an investigation into social worlds and class (Vassenden and Jonvik, 2022), an enquiry into the fatigue experienced by children aged between 12 and 17 with sickle cell anaemia (Poku et al, 2019), a project relating to participants' involvement in college-based outdoor programmes (Loeffler, 2004), a study into the physical setting of a hospital ward and its role in patients' recovery (Radley and Taylor, 2003), and the exploration of classroom-based learning experiences of children aged 4 and 5 (Pyle, 2013). In effect, this approach is used across a vast range of participants in a wide variety of settings and disciplinary contexts in order to answer a realm of research questions.

The basis for this approach again lies with the role of photography as a 'can-opener' (Collier and Collier, 1986, p 25), but rather than requiring the researcher identify and select photographs, the participants are asked to supply the images. Research articles largely describe how participants were asked to provide images, with some even sharing some of the prompts provided (see Chapter 2 example from Hatten et al, 2013). For example, Alvariza et al (2020) describe how they instructed nurses to take three photographs ahead of their interview of what they found to be important to them in the home care environment. The nurses were offered the option to take those photographs using their personal smart phones or they were supplied with a digital camera. The authors also describe how the photographs were transferred to a computer and displayed on the computer screen during the interview. Pyle (2013) describes that in the project with very young children, the children were tasked with taking two photographs of their most important places, activities, and/or people in their classroom environment. The restricted number of photographs resulted in more carefully selected and higher-quality images, as children went back to retake their pictures if they were not completely satisfied. In the group interview following the photography task, the images were shared with the children by placing five to ten photographs on the floor. The children were then able to discuss these photographs before another set of five to ten photographs was introduced. This process was repeated until the full class set of photographs was discussed. The outlines of these two examples lead quite naturally into the consideration of how to implement the method in practice.

Implementing the method

For most research using photovoice as method with participant-supplied photographs, the point of departure is the desire to explore participants' perceptions, experiences, thoughts, and opinions. To this end, researchers then ask their participants to supply photographs showing and representing particular elements of those experiences and perceptions. Here are some key areas to be considered when planning a project using photovoice as method with participant-supplied photographs.

1. The design of a prompt

For participants to be able to supply meaningful photographs for the interview, they will need to be provided with guidance on what they are asked to do. Designing a prompt sounds easy enough, in principle, but we all have experienced occasions where our questions were misinterpreted or where our instructions were misunderstood. The development of a prompt requires significant planning and quite detailed understanding of the target participants. Questions we may ask ourselves here are: How many photographs should be brought? Can the photographs be 'found', thus taken from the internet or a magazine or do they have to be specifically generated? Do the photographs need captions or commentaries and if texts are required what form or format do they have to take? What size do the images need to be and which format; that is, do they have to be digital or can they be prints? What should the photographs show?

In relation to this last question, we need to consider if the participants require some guidance on how to take a photograph. Some researchers talk about specific training or prompts they offer to their participants, in order to ensure that they are taking photographs ethically. For the study on the impact of the physical space of a hospital ward on patients' recovery, for example, participants were told

> that the pictures could be of anything on the ward that was significant to them – these might be positive or negative things. They might select spaces, things that were part of the hospital, or objects that they had brought in with them. (Radley and Taylor, 2003, p 81)

By asking their participants to focus on spaces, things, and objects, the researchers avoided the ethical consideration of having to ask people for permission to have their photograph taken. When there was no specific guidance for participants what the pictures should be of in a study of outdoor experiences, approximately a third of the pictures submitted involved people, such as friends, friendship groups, and group leaders (Loeffler, 2004). Unfortunately, how this was treated ethically and if these other individuals were asked for permissions does not become clear in the published report.

Another issue relates to photography as a skill. Some target participants will be very confident using their own personal cameras or smart phones; other target populations may only have limited experience with photography and potentially not even own a camera or camera-enabled phone. Participants having little experience or confidence with photography may draw on others to assist them, which potentially has repercussions for the kind of data that are collected and for what the data represent. In the photovoice study with older adults exploring the age-friendliness of their communities, for example, some participants asked to take photographs on an individual basis actually undertook the task jointly with their spouses (Novek et al, 2012). Receiving data from couples, rather than individuals, offered unexpected insights into participants' joint lives, but at the same time left the researchers wondering about whose voice was represented.

In my own work with people diagnosed with fibromyalgia, I used creative methods to explore how individuals make sense of their academic identity under the influence of fibromyalgia. The pilot phase focused on non-academic members of the public, whereas the full study was with academics at different stages of their careers. The main approach to data collection was the generation of a box of objects in response to questions I had asked. Participants were then required to take a photograph of the box with the objects and send it to me with a brief note of what I would see in the picture before the next question was released (see www.nicole-brown.co.uk/?s=fibromyalgia for more details). This project was not designed as a photovoice study, but the ethical, methodological, and practical considerations were the same. And I found that you can never provide too much guidance regarding the taking of the photograph and that more support is always beneficial. Initially, I had not included any stipulations regarding the photographs in my prompts. I soon realised my mistake when I started receiving images that were out of focus (see Figure 3.2) and poorly lit (see Figure 3.3). In such instances I was

Figure 3.2: Participant Ch's photograph of the exterior of their identity box

Figure 3.3: Participant L1's photograph of the interior of their identity box

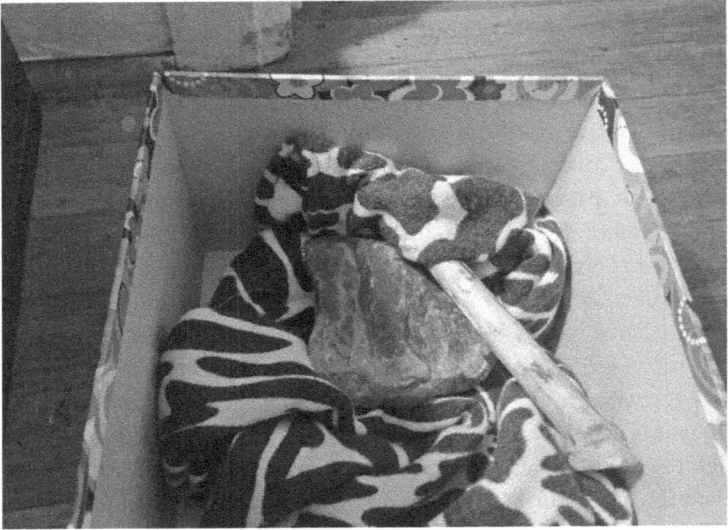

only able to identify the objects in the box from the participant-generated texts that accompanied the photographs.

The project was designed such that I would begin my analytical process to interpret the photographs before scheduling the interview with the participants. It was therefore important for me to see and recognise the objects placed in the boxes, and I had to ask my participants to retake the photographs. To remedy the issue, I decided to revise my prompt. I recorded a short video of me talking about the quality of the photographs and what to look out for in an image. I uploaded that video as an unlisted entry on YouTube and shared the link with all my participants. This is the video, where I explain how I would like the photographs to be taken: www.youtube.com/watch?v=cafNG6Xw33o. Of course, the prompt could have been written, but with my target participants struggling with cognitive issues, also known as brain fog, due to their fibromyalgia diagnosis, I felt that a written prompt was not the best choice.

Another aspect to consider relates to the time frame of the data collection. On the one hand, participants will need to be given enough time to be able to explore their lived experience and their lifeworld using cameras, as they may not ever have done that before in such a way. On the other hand, however, the time frame cannot be too long, as the participants will feel like they have lost touch with the project and the researcher. In my fibromyalgia study, I initially suggested a one-week time frame for each photograph, but then let myself be guided by the participants. Some participants honoured the one-week deadline; others took three times as long for the same project.

2. Planning for the sharing of photographs

If as researchers we are asking our participants to create photographs, we need to plan for how the images are shared and in what context. Some form of sharing will happen between the participant and the researcher, as digital photographs are transferred from cameras to laptops. Some sharing also takes place in the interview situation, which may be separate from or coincide with the digital image transfer. Questions to consider here are: Do the participants need to share their pictures ahead of the interview? Do the photographs need to be shared as prints or in digital form? How can data be transferred and transmitted safely and securely? How and when are photographs removed from the researcher's computer? What happens to printed photographs? Who gets to keep and use the digital/printed photographs? Some of these questions are of a practical nature, as they make us consider the size of the photographs and storage space needed. That may mean that a simple email with attachment will not work, as the photographs become too big. But can we actually rely on our target participants to have access to email and internet? Some of the questions refer to ethical issues and concerns, especially around ownership, copyright, and right of use (for more on practical and ethical considerations, see Chapter 6).

3. Planning the interview questions relating to the photographs

Ensuring the photographs are useful and meaningful, as well as shared safely, securely, and ethically, is only half the battle.

Photovoice as a method with participant-supplied photographs requires the opportunity for researchers to talk to their participants about the photographs. Many photovoice studies revert here to what has entered common discourse as the SHOWeD technique. Drawing on Wallerstein (1987) and Shaffer (1984), Wang (1999) uses the acronym SHOWeD in relation to the questions researchers should ask in order to facilitate the participants' story-telling and sense-making. The original questions are:

> What do you **S**ee here?
> What is really **H**appening here?
> How does this relate to **O**ur lives?
> **W**hy does this situation, concern, or strength exist?
> What can we **D**o about it? (Wang, 1999, p 188, emphasis in original)

With the photovoice as a method approach focusing somewhat less on the transformative nature of the research, researchers tend to move away from the last two questions, change the original questions to better suit their target participants, or use an adapted version popularised by the National Association of City & County Health Officials (Sutton-Brown, 2014; Werremeyer et al, 2020). Effectively, photovoice must be treated like any other interview study, where we must design the interview questions appropriately to ensure we obtain the data we need and want for our research purposes.

Advantages and drawbacks of the method

In publications researchers using photovoice as a method with participant-supplied photographs tend to emphasise the benefit of the individuality of the participant data. As the participants are supplying the images, the photographs are particularly meaningful and refer to each participant's personality and individuality in ways that researcher-supplied photographs cannot. Within educational research, the individuality of data has been seen helpful in offering highly contextualised insights, which would otherwise be difficult to achieve (Hidalgo Standen, 2021). For researchers engaging in this approach, the variety of photographs submitted is also not problematic, as the data come from the sense-making with the participants in interviews rather than from the photographs themselves. What tends to be focused on more is how the approach is experienced as engaging or enjoyable (for example, Close, 2007; Cook and Hess, 2007; Whiting, 2015), and how, therefore, this approach is particularly suited for researchers to build rapport with their participants. However, when it comes to generated photographs, there will need to be sufficient guidance from the researchers to ensure that participants are aware of the kinds of images they can take without risking potential disclosures and to ensure no non-consenting individuals are pictured.

Another advantage of this approach is that participants may be able to draw on images from the internet, magazines, newspapers, advertisements, or their existing personal collections rather than having to generate their own photographs. The photographs in this approach are generally a stimulus for conversation rather than a data set to be analysed or disseminated. Thus, researchers do not have to insist on participants producing images. By allowing participants to use found images, the process that is often described as time-consuming becomes somewhat more time-efficient and convenient (Allen, 2020). A downside for the use of found images is that the use of these photographs will be restricted when it comes to sharing in publications, for example, as the photographers or website owners or magazine publishers will own the rights to the photographs. Finally, with found photographs neither the researchers nor the participants will know about the exact origins, background, and other contextual details of the selected pre-existing images (Pauwels, 2010). This is where the design of the photovoice study again becomes crucial. If the aim is to enable conversation and have participants illustrate their experiences, then the illustrative value of the photographs can be exploited in the conversations between participants and researchers, irrespective of how the images came to be. If, however, the visual materials are seen as a valuable insight into how society is presented and represented (Pauwels, 2010), then contextualisation is key and found images will not be suitable. This is where the conceptualisation of photovoice as framework comes in.

Photovoice as a framework

In Chapters 1 and 2, I offered an outline of how photovoice as a framework emerged from anthropological and ethnographic documentary work with the term photovoice ultimately becoming popular in the 1990s. With its emphasis on participant engagement for active transformation, photovoice as framework sits at the right end of the continuum (see Figure 3.1). Photovoice as a framework connects several key concepts:

> Concept 1: Images teach
> Concept 2: Pictures can influence policy
> Concept 3: Community people ought to participate in creating and defining the images that shape healthful public policy
> Concept 4: The process requires that planners bring to the table from the outset policy makers and other influential people to serve as an audience for community people's perspectives
> Concept 5: Photovoice emphasizes individual and community action (Wang, 1999, pp 186–7)

Originally, photovoice as a framework was developed with a feminist stance in mind and so it was expected the participants and community people to be women.

> By women telling their and their communities' stories, we might better understand the context that women confer on their lives and health conditions. (Wang, 1999, p 186)

As the approach became used more widely, the feminist underpinning gave way to the understanding that photovoice should be used with all oppressed and marginalised populations. Even the originator herself reported on a photovoice study involving men as well as women with the argument that

> homeless people in Washtenaw County, as in many other communities, are a highly stigmatized group with

minimal access to the media or to the policy makers whose decisions influence their lives. (Wang, 1998, p 9)

In research employing photovoice as a framework, the participants are asked to provide images relating to their experiences, which they will then make sense of in group discussions facilitated by a researcher. The photographs are central to the social change agenda and the endeavour to highlight gaps, misgivings, and injustices. The subsequent group discussions, then, enable the participants to formulate recommendations and strategies for action that are to be shared with relevant stakeholders and policy makers. In the following section I provide more detail regarding these individual steps to implement photovoice as a framework.

Implementing the method

When photovoice is used as a framework, it should ideally follow the steps originally outlined in the 1990s:

> Select and recruit a target audience of policymakers or community leaders
> Recruit a group of photovoice participants
> Introduce the photovoice methodology to participants and facilitate a group discussion
> Obtain informed consent
> Pose an initial theme for taking pictures
> Distribute cameras to participants and review how to use them
> Provide time for participants to take pictures
> Meet to discuss photographs
> Plan with participants a format to share photographs and stories with policymakers or community leaders. (Wang, 1999, pp 187–9)

By following this detailed process researchers can ensure that participants are, at least to an extent, trained in research skills as well as in taking photographs effectively and ethically, while also focusing on the participatory and transformative nature of the approach. Further, the guidance suggests the recruitment of between seven and ten participants for the group discussion with sampling being either purposive or random. The group size of seven to ten is recommended for the discussions to remain in-depth as well as manageable, while at the same time enabling researchers to select participants from a wider demographic range, if that is needed.

The key to successful photovoice projects is to spend significant amounts of time on facilitating training. Not only are the researchers fostering research and photography skills in their participants, they are also enabling community leaders, policy makers, and other influential stakeholders to get a deeper insight into participants' experiences. Although stakeholders are not involved in the bulk of the project (they are only mentioned at the beginning and at the very end), they play an important role in the function as target audience. In effect, the stakeholders are used as an advisory board or consultants. Participants can trial presenting their stories and photographs along with their recommendations to the stakeholders. The influential stakeholders, in turn, are expected to offer feedback to the participants but also by taking forward these recommendations to the relevant decision-making entity. Consequently, the recruitment of stakeholders is purposive with inclusion criteria relating to the potential stakeholders' sphere of influence, decision-making powers, and political will to engage with transformation and to act on recommendations.

While the recruitment and involvement of influential stakeholders and relevant agencies is an undisputed element in ensuring the success of photovoice (Wang and Pies, 2004; Foster-Fishman et al, 2005), there is criticism regarding the timing of the stakeholder recruitment. Sutton-Brown (2014) argues that the participant-led agenda of photovoice is undermined if the researchers purposively select stakeholders at the beginning of a project, as that recruitment would be based purely on the researchers' preconceptions and theories. Instead, the stakeholder recruitment should be moved to after the sharing of the photographs in group discussions. This would ensure that the participants themselves could stipulate some of the inclusion and exclusion criteria for the recruitment process. As a result, the participants' decision-making agency would remain intact, as the stakeholder engagement would emerge more directly from the participants' stories and photographs.

The practical implementation of photovoice as a framework is generally widely critiqued in scoping reviews and systematic reviews. Overall, most reviews recognise the value of photographs along with participant involvement during data collection, as well as the admirable aim of photovoice projects to bring about change. However, findings show low levels of stakeholder engagement, limited impact of participants within dissemination, poor evaluation of policy changes brought about by photovoice, limited reporting on photovoice processes around ethics, and the glossing over of how photovoice is implemented in practice (Hergenrather et al, 2009; Catalani and Minkler, 2010; Han and Oliffe, 2016; Derr and Simons, 2020; Seitz and Orsini, 2022). In one review (Sanon et al, 2014), only three of the 30 studies reviewed had reported significant transformation and social change within the participants' communities, even though many other studies referred to the awareness-raising effects of their photovoice research. This quite naturally brings us to considering the advantages and drawbacks of photovoice.

Advantages and drawbacks of the method

In my experience, the biggest advantage of photovoice as a framework is at the same time its biggest drawback: the community engagement. Undoubtedly, there is a significant benefit in engaging members of local communities as participants in research affecting their immediate settings and contexts. However, the real impact of photovoice on the communities, its transformative nature, is hardly ever assessed formally. By focusing on the community-driven and problem-based characteristics, research using photovoice as a framework becomes particularly time-consuming. Just like in all other highly participatory approaches to research, there is also a risk that the participant-led agenda moves a research project into unforeseen, unplanned, and potentially unwanted directions. In the context of participatory and creative research methods, I have long argued that researchers should not strive for fully egalitarian and participatory research because of the potential risk to participants running into harm (Brown, 2022a). Indeed, this risk is much greater when participants work in a group and making collective decisions.

In the context of the contemporary research landscape, community engagement poses a challenge in other ways.

Community engagement, decolonisation, inclusion of Indigenous populations, and links with the Global South may be high on the agenda of current research. However, most research requires funding from higher education institutions or grant providers. These, in turn, require proposals written by researchers that are then evaluated for their originality, contribution, rigour, as well as value for money. Proposals are therefore most often developed and written independently of local communities. By default, there is tension between the development of research proposals and the photovoice requirement to include communities in the agenda setting and to draw on participants' experiences to identify gaps to be plugged and concerns to be addressed.

On the continuum of photovoice

Considering the benefits and pitfalls of photovoice as a method and photovoice as a framework, it is probably no longer surprising that there are so many variations described in research. Photovoice is nowadays well recognised as a feasible approach to strengthen research, especially where interventionist agendas are important, such as in education or health (Catalani and Minkler, 2010; Seitz and Orsini, 2022). In practice, however, the reviews show that photovoice

> can vary across key stages, including training, research and documentation, and photo-elicited discussion. (Catalani and Minkler, 2010, p 448)

In short, the settings and contexts of research, the participant demographic, the research foci, and questions all impact the design of a photovoice study. Most researchers find themselves sliding along the continuum of photovoice with encouraging more community engagement in some areas and holding on more tightly to responsibility and control over the research in others. Also, what may work for one project does not necessarily suit another. As a consequence, researchers position themselves on different points of the continuum from one research project to the next. In the following chapters relating to analysis and dissemination I will show that most of my work sits somewhere between photovoice as method with participant-supplied photographs and photovoice as a framework.

End of chapter tasks

1. Return to the research question you formulated in Chapter 2 and assume you are now planning a project. You want to use photovoice as method with participant-supplied photographs. Design the prompt(s) for your participants. In your journal, try to respond to your own prompt(s).

2. Use the research question you formulated in Chapter 2 and take ten photographs relating to that question. From this set of ten images, select three photographs you deem most suitable. Make a note of how you made your choice. Finally, using the SHOWeD template, notice how you explain your photograph and how you justify the choices you have made.

4

Photovoice in and as analysis

Chapter aims

- To demystify the analysis of photographs.

- To consider the analysis of photographs in combination with texts.

- To introduce the creation of photographs as an analytical process.

Introduction

In the previous chapters I focused on the origins of photovoice, the design of photovoice research, and the implementation of photovoice in and as data collection. I now build on these foundations in order to discuss analytical approaches and questions. How data analysis within photovoice is approached depends on the researcher's view of whether the photographs are considered as data.

Researchers may consider photographs purely as an opportunity to deepen participants' reflections and enter a conversation. In this case, photographs are topics in interviews with the researcher asking participants to comment on what they see and how the images relate to their personal experiences, perceptions, thoughts, and feelings. However, the photographs do not feature as a separate set of data. The data in such a project remain the interview, and the researcher will not interpret or analyse photographs.

Researchers may also view the photographs as forms of expression that have an important function for the communication of ideas in addition to what participants are sharing verbally. The philosophical and theoretical foundations for this view lie with the acknowledgement that language is insufficient and inexact when it comes to expressing detailed experiences (Scarry, 1985; Sontag, 2003) and that human communication is therefore metaphorical (Lakoff and Johnson, 2003) (cf. 'Embodied Inquiry' in Chapter 2). Based on this recognition, photographs are data. Consequently, researchers need to consider how they can incorporate the participant-supplied or -generated images into their analytical process. However, in my research methods workshops and training sessions, I notice that for many researchers wanting to engage in photovoice projects the prospect of analysing visuals is often experienced as too daunting. Workshop delegates recognise their limitations when it comes to approaching visuals and tend to ask for practical strategies and steps for doing analysis of photographs. In the following, I would like to offer three distinct opportunities:

(1) researchers may analyse the images as visual materials;
(2) researchers may analyse photographs in combination with the textual data; and
(3) researchers may engage in developing visual materials as part of an analytical process.

Before I dive into these three sections, I would like to take a moment to reflect on why researchers using photographs in their projects may shy away from interpreting, thus analysing photographs. I will then outline the process of analysing photographs and discuss the analysis of text and photograph. After the section on developing photographs as an analytical process, I take the opportunity to consider participant involvement within analysis.

Reflections on analysing photographs

For many researchers the analysis of photographs comes with worries around over-interpretation and insecurities relating to the ability to interpret. These anxieties are often compounded by the technical language of linguistics (the study of language), semiotics (the study of the use of symbolic communication), and semiology (the study of sign processes and meaning-making) introduced in many visual methods handbooks (see, for example, van Leeuwen and Jewitt, 2001; ; Spencer, 2010; Margolis and Pauwels, 2011; Machin, 2014; Pauwels and Mannay, 2019; Ledin and Machin, 2018; Rose, 2023).

Interestingly, when asked about these same issues relating to interview transcripts and how these same researchers may know when they have over-interpreted a text, they can often not explain the lines and boundaries, but they definitely feel much more confident. It appears that through socialisation in research contexts, researchers have gained significant experience with the interpretation of text and have had opportunities to discuss coding and theme-finding based on interview transcripts, while the consideration of images and photographs becomes sidelined. Additionally, when attempting to analyse a photograph, researchers often struggle to identify what they can interpret. In effect, when looking at a photograph, they have quickly jumped to conclusions, thus interpreted the image, without realising that these are already interpretative thoughts.

The photograph in Figure 4.1 comes from my research project relating to representations of identity and memories. The project's premise is that handbags or rucksacks can obviously be used as fashion accessories or statements (Savi, 2020), but that they also fulfil practical purposes, such as being financial centres, communication hubs, pharmacy, cosmetic counters, and storage for objects of sentimental value (Styring, 2007). As such, a person knowingly or unknowingly expresses their identity and memories through the kinds of handbags and rucksacks they use and the objects the bags contain. Let us consider the participant photograph (see Figure 4.1). What do you see?

When asked what they see in the photograph, researchers often respond along the lines of "this is the clutch of a woman, who …". This is already an interpretation. The picture shows objects strewn on the floor, with the objects being earplugs, contact lens container, cough sweets, a small bottle of essential oils, some medication, a mini-sewing kit, and tissues. There is no woman shown in the photograph, nor is there any comment stating that

Figure 4.1: Participant photograph of a handbag

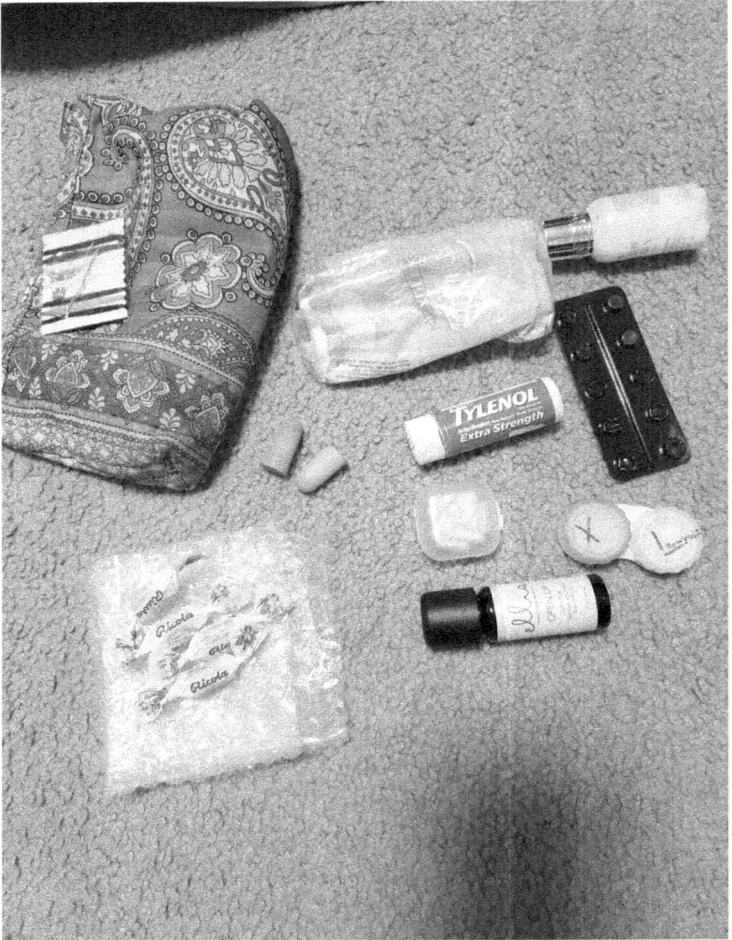

the participant is a woman, nor is there a statement claiming the contents belong to a woman. We do not *see* a woman's clutch; we interpret the clutch as belonging to a woman. As it happens, this participant is a woman, but that is beside the point, here. The point is that, once we have interpreted this clutch as a woman's clutch, we have nowhere else to go in our interpretations. That jump from seeing an image to this level of interpretation happens so quickly that we are often not even aware of having made connections that are situated at an interpretative rather than on a descriptive level. In our everyday lives, we are consistently exposed to images, and so we have learned to analyse visual materials in a split second. Instead of worrying about our abilities to interpret photographs, we need to relearn the way we view images by slowing down the process. Instead of asking ourselves what a photograph tells us and then becoming confused about why we cannot analyse what we see, we should break down task into two separate questions: What do I see? And what do I make of it? Using Figure 4.1 as an example, what we see is a clutch with objects – cough sweets, a small bottle of essential oils, some medication, a mini-sewing kit, and so on – next to it. What we make of it is that this clutch belongs to a woman (clutch, in the original photo it is pink, but you will see it in a shade of grey) who has some visual impairment (contact lens container), who prefers quiet spaces (earplugs), and who has a cough or dry throat (cough sweets).

The accurateness of this interpretation, thus the quality of our analysis, is nearly impossible to judge, as we do not have any contextual details. This is another concern researchers mention, when considering if they would like to use photographs as data or not. In the previous example, we saw the clutch, which we felt looks feminine, and so we concluded that the owner is a woman. As I mentioned, in this case, the owner is indeed a woman. Yet, we do need to acknowledge that our assumptions, biases, and prior experiences will shape what we make of a photograph, and that therefore our interpretation may not be entirely accurate. However, how is this different from interpreting text? Is it not true that when we interpret what participants said in interviews, we also add layers of our own assumptions, biases, and prior experiences and view that interview transcript through that particular lens? It is not my intention to raise doubt and cause further anxieties. Instead, I am trying to show that as we are confident in our abilities to interpret text, so we can be confident in analysing photographs.

Analysing photographs

As the relevance of photographs within research has long been recognised, there are many textbooks and analytical frameworks exploring how to analyse photographs. Some scholars writing about the analysis of images focus on the analysis of the visuals per se (for example, Gleeson, 2011; Chapman et al, 2017). Other commentators emphasise the understanding that images and visual materials are also forms of texts, and therefore can be analysed in the same way as textual data is analysed (for example, Braun and Clarke, 2011; Ritchie et al, 2014). Each of these frameworks, along with many others not mentioned here, underlies specific philosophical and theoretical foundations that shape the ultimate design, process, and interpretation of the analytical process itself. In the final write-up of a research, these foundations need to be explored, explained, and justified, of course. It will, therefore, be useful for any researcher considering visual analysis to delve deeper into the matter before getting stuck in with the analytical process. However, although the individual processes and philosophical underpinnings differ from one another, there are some basic procedural elements that combine nearly all texts. For the sake of clarity and concision, I call these three stages immersion, coding, and interpretation.

Immersion

The first stage in the process of analysing photographs as data requires the researcher to immerse themselves in that data. Some scholars describe this phase as 'open' and 'unstructured' (Collier and Collier, 1986, p 181). This phase corresponds to the familiarisation stage of textual analysis. In this phase, we look through the photographs that have been submitted, catalogue them, index them, and write descriptions of them. The question we ask here is: "What do I see?" At this stage, there is no particular focus for how to view photographs. But drawing on the theories of visual communication and visual arts, we may want to think about the composition of each photograph, lights, colours, or about the themes they represent. Immersing ourselves into that photographic data will enable us then to create different sets of photographs depending on what we notice. The initial engagement with the data in this open and unstructured way, therefore, gradually leads into the next phase, where we do begin the sense-making process more earnestly.

Coding

Although my classifications here suggest clear delineations between the different phases, the moving from immersion to coding is often quite organic. At one point, when looking at our photographic data, we realise that we are starting to ask more definitive questions of what the data show, or we begin to focus on particular themes. This natural move away from the open and unstructured viewing in the immersion stage is a good indication for us to recognise that we are sufficiently familiar with our data and that we can formally begin coding. Thus, this phase of analysing photographs relates to the question: "What do I make of this?" By entering the interpretative realm of a photograph's meaning, we are able to identify and assign meaningful labels to what the data show. This is coding. Depending on the overall research design, coding may either draw on a priori codes, on free codes, or on a combination of the two, just as it would within textual analysis. In the context of analysing photographs, the a priori codes to be used may come from existing research, from theory developed and created for the purpose of the research on hand, or from what participants have said in interviews. Coding then is nothing else but recognising that there is a relationship between our theories, previous research, or participants' statements, and the photographic data set we deal with. In practice, most researchers code using a list of codes created a priori along with the free coding that will inevitably happen along the way because photographs depict elements of experiences that had not been predicted. As a result, working through photographs, we end up with a large number of codes. At this stage, however, the meaning, relevance, and role of these codes remain somewhat elusive. It is our task to reduce those codes into manageable quantities of meaningful labels. This is where we enter the final stage: interpretation.

Interpretation

In the context of textual analysis, there is eventually a process described that allows us to turn many codes into a small number of themes. Although it often appears linear, this condensing of codes into themes is a cyclical process of alternating between open coding, axial coding, and selective coding. Where open codes allow for the identification of broad key terms, axial coding refines these initial labels so that during selective coding the researcher can select, combine, and integrate the respective terms to make a coherent theme (Williams and Moser, 2019, pp 48–54). This interpretation stage of the analytical process, therefore, requires us researchers to 'wander backwards and forwards' (Collier and Collier, 1986, p 100), to weave our way from the individual codes through the condensed codes to potential themes, and back to verify and review the interpretations.

Analysis of photographs: a worked example

The following image (see Figure 4.2) is a participant-generated photograph that I received from K, one of my participants in my fibromyalgia study. I was exploring the lived experience of academics with fibromyalgia and, to this end, I had introduced the identity boxes (see Chapter 3). However, some participants supplied additional materials, such as narratives or photographs,

Figure 4.2: Participant K's photograph of the 'lived experience of fibromyalgia'

to provide further, more detailed expressions of their experiences with fibromyalgia.

In the first stage, the immersion stage, we focus on what we see in the image: I can see a person's feet clothed in thick socks sticking out from under fabric (in the original photo it is blue-coloured). From the way the shadows act, I can see that there must be a light source outside the image. I can see a white radiator behind a thin, white, long curtain. It appears that the feet are at a different height to the carpeted floor. I can see something textured (in the original photo it is a reddish-brownish colour).

The next two stages are then the coding and interpretation stages, where we consider what we can make of what we see. In this particular worked example, we do not know of any a priori codes, so we need to try and identify some codes from the image: I make of this image that there is someone having a rest on a sofa chair or sofa, that they are feeling quite cold, which is why I can see the thick socks and blue sleeping bag, and that this is in the evening, which is why there is an artificial light source outside the picture. The terms 'resting', 'cold/warm', and 'light/dark' are therefore my first codes.

With these initial codes, we are now turning to other images to identify the relevance of those codes. Figure 4.3 is a collage of further images K supplied.

The process for these photographs is the same, in that we begin with the immersion phase before entering the coding phase. However, at this stage we are now working with the codes we have already generated from the previous image (see Figure 4.2). We are now considering the relevance of 'resting', 'cold/warm', and 'light/dark'. This is now the interpretation phase, where the codes are gradually turned into themes. And it does become

Figure 4.3: Participant K's photograph collection of the 'lived experience of fibromyalgia'

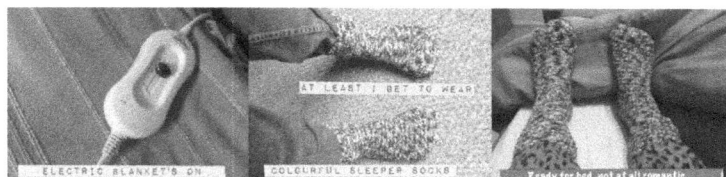

obvious that 'cold/warm' is an important element. This leads to the conclusion that in this participant's lived experience of fibromyalgia, there is a tendency to feel cold, which results in the need to counteract this coldness with measures for keeping warm. We have now firmly entered the interpretation phase of the analytical process. At this stage, the analysis needs to be continued across all the data across all participants. In this case, it became evident that the experience of warmth and cold plays a significant role in how pain symptoms within fibromyalgia are aggravated and relieved.

About the analysis of texts and photographs

Largely, as the previous sections would have shown, the analysis of photographs aligns with how we code and create themes when analysing interview transcripts. The significant difference I have encountered relates to intentionality and purpose. Let me use another example from my research into the construction of academic identity under the influence of fibromyalgia.

Figure 4.4 is the photograph participant L2 submitted to me in response to the question: "Who are you?" The accompanying email explained that the card in the centre of the box represented L2's role as a family-orientated homemaker. The card was therefore coded as 'family' and 'homemaker'. Figure 4.5 is the photograph participant L2 submitted to me in response to the question, "What affects you?", after L2 had added a number of items to the previous artefacts.

Given the design of the project, I had expected the objects from previous weeks to be inside the box, and so I would have expected to see the card I had coded 'homemaker', 'family'. However, during my immersion phase, I had noticed that the card that had been on the bottom of the box in Week 1 was propped up against the side in Week 2. By the time I entered the interpretation stage, and I needed to (re)consider the codes in order to identify relevant themes, the positioning of the card became a key consideration. When we analyse texts drawn from interview transcripts, we can reasonably assume that the participants communicate what they express with a particular level of intentionality. Potentially, participants are not entirely truthful; maybe they withhold specific

Figure 4.4: Participant L2's photograph of the interior of her identity box (Week 1)

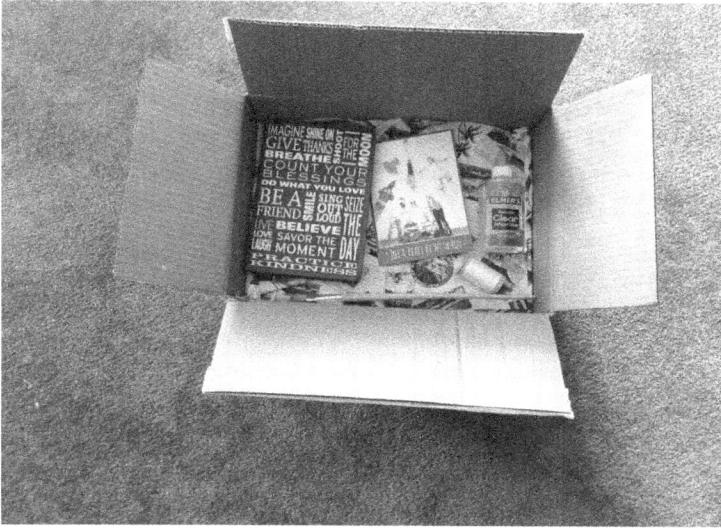

Figure 4.5: Participant L2's photograph of the interior of her identity box (Week 2)

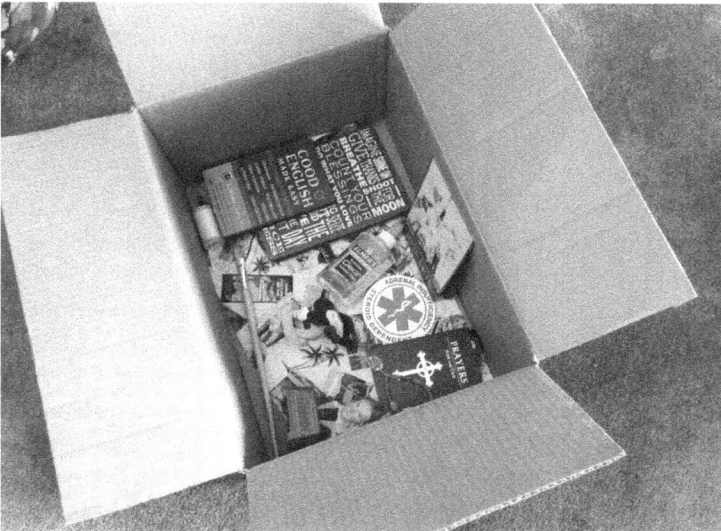

information, but whatever they communicate, they communicate purposefully. When it comes to photography, the photographer's intentions of and with a photograph may be less easy to recognise. As for Figures 4.4 and 4.5, could it be that L2 had positioned the family, homemaker card deliberately on the side of the box so that the codes family and homemaker were relevant for the question in week 2 as well as in week 1? Was L2 trying to say that being a family-orientated homemaker was something that affected her? Could it be that the card was placed randomly, but would it then stand up against the side of the box? Was there possibly another, entirely different, reason for why L2 had positioned the card the way she had? All answers to these questions would be possible, reasonable, meaningful, and relevant. And they would shape how the codes are dealt with in the subsequent interpretative stages of theme generation. Yet, from the images alone, we have no way of knowing for sure. There are two ways of dealing with this conundrum: incorporate the uncertainty around intentionality into the interpretation or ask the participant. The latter brings me to the question of how we can combine the analysis of visuals and texts in a systematic manner.

Analysing texts and photographs

As the number of projects using photovoice as a method with participant-supplied photographs increases, there is a more pronounced need for a way to combine the analysis of texts and photographs. In recent years, several frameworks have been published that use the relationship between texts and images in similar, yet slightly different, ways. The framework by Grange and Lian (2022) focuses on the text–image relation according to Roland Barthes. The textual-visual thematic analysis by Trombeta and Cox (2022), by contrast, emphasises guiding questions to help steer the analysis of photographs in relation to texts. The third framework to be mentioned in this context is the systematic visuo-textual analysis that primarily focuses on how to connect textual data and visual data without prioritising one mode over the other (Brown and Collins, 2021). While these frameworks may differ in their philosophical view of what constitutes an image and how the relationship between image and text is to be seen, the procedural steps are very much aligned. All authors emphasise the need for the continuous iteration of 'wander[ing] backwards and forwards' (Collier and Collier, 1986, p 100) not only between codes, but also between the text and the images. The process of analysis in all three frameworks requires the researchers to code and identify themes of interview transcripts, to code and identify themes in photographs, and to then compare and contrast the two sets of findings. As such, all frameworks require the researchers to engage in a prolonged, iterative process.

Within the scope of text–image relations analysis (Grange and Lian, 2022) or the systematic visuo-textual analysis (Brown and Collins, 2021), this iterative process is achieved by comparing data within the cases, between cases and at different levels of interpretation. Specifically, researchers are asked to 'weave from one element and level to the next' (Brown and Collins, 2021, p 1281). How to do this is described in the open-access article about the systematic visuo-textual analysis, where we offer a worked example applying the framework to LEGO® models and interrelated interviews (Brown and Collins, 2021). In their study about teacher interns' lived experience during the COVID-19 pandemic, Cheryl Burleigh, Andrea Wilson, and Jim Lane explain:

> The process of reviewing the textual content that accompanied each photo provided a rich description of how the specific image directly related to the context in which the photo was presented. [...] As we analyzed the interrelated and entwined visual and textual data, we developed a clearer and deeper understanding of the experiences of everyone. Cheryl and Andrea independently analyzed the narrative and visual data for commonalities and categories through resonant images. They then shared and merged their analyses. Although the participants' visual and narrative reflections were idiosyncratic we were surprised at the continuity that flowed across stories and images. (Burleigh et al, 2022, p 1588)

As is evident the process of the analysis remains described quite loosely, even though the steps described in the frameworks offer an insight into how combining texts with images may work in practice.

Trombeta and Cox (2022), by contrast, propose specific questions, which researchers should ask of themselves and their data:

> What is in the images that supports or reinforces what was learned from the interview data?
> What is in the images that contradicts what was learned from the interview data?
> What is in the images that is not in the interviews?
> What is in the interviews that is not in the images?
> (Trombeta and Cox, 2022, p 1566)

If we look carefully at these questions, we can see how difficult it is to ensure that both, texts and images, are considered of equal value and are not set as better or more important than the other. In this particular case, the interview transcripts seem to be taking a slightly more prominent positioning, as the images are set directly against and in comparison to transcripts. In describing the systematic visuo-textual analysis, by contrast, Brown and Collins (2021) highlight that the framework does not prescribe a particular order of analysis. Instead, they recommend deciding on the order of an analytical process, thus if textual or visual analysis comes first, by considering the contexts of a research.

What will have become evident is that by incorporating the analysis of photographs into the analysis of texts or vice versa, the analytical process becomes more strenuous and time-consuming. Although photographs and interview transcripts may only constitute two sets of data, a combined or joint analysis takes more than twice as long because of the connections that need to be made between the separate analyses. With the frameworks being relatively new within the academic realm, there have also been few critiques published to date. And so far, none of the frameworks explore how to deal with contradictions or how to navigate the space between researcher-interpretations and participant-interpretations, which do not necessarily overlap. In the previously mentioned example from my own research, I asked participant L2 about the role of the photocard in the identity box within the scope of member-checking, which is commonly applied in qualitative research. In this sense, the analytical process becomes extended by another feature, the returning to the participants with specific questions to be clarified. That contact does not need to be of the length of another full interview, but can be a very quick check-in. Approaching the participants with such questions will enhance the robustness and validity of the interpretations, while also enabling insights that would probably not be gained without this brief member-check.

Photographs as analysis

When we consider analysis in qualitative research, we quite naturally tend to think about coding and theme generation, about moving from the individual transcript across all data sets to the generic, more widely applicable. To understand the role of generalisability, transferability, causality, truthfulness, and/or verisimilitude in qualitative research, I would urge you to read widely to transcend the disciplinary conventions of your own research context (for example, Hammersley, 2007; Tracy, 2010; Barone and Eisner, 2011; Leavy, 2015, 2020; Flick, 2018). Irrespective of where we sit in the debate of generalisability and the like, analysis in its rudimentary kind is a form of understanding and interpreting data, thus a process of sense-making. It just so happens that we tend to be able to do that systematically if we are using labels that we attach to the data, which we can then extract, organise, review, and reorganise. In short, this is what I described earlier, a process of immersion, coding, and interpretation. However, this form of sense-making is not the only way we make sense of situations or experiences as human beings. In our everyday lives, we may be drawing mind-maps, we may doodle, or we may simply think things through. Well, this is what we can do in research contexts, too. Instead of analysing photographs as data sets in their own rights with or without the links to texts, we can use photography and the power of photographs to help us understand our data. The purposeful creation of photographs as individual sets of work, as series, or as a collage will enable us to access our data in a different way. I do not propose to use photographs as analysis without considering the more conventional forms of analysis, simply because of the potential repercussions relating to publications and career prospects. Yet, I do encourage researchers to engage with the process of photograph generation for analytical purposes. The generation of our own photographs taps into a different form of sense-making than the conventional coding. Through thinking about and then actually creating our own photograph, we engage with our embodiment, our emotions, our experiences, and our responses to the data in front of us. In addition, the process of thinking about staging a photograph, then taking that picture to review it, allows us to gain a much better understanding of what our participants experience, when we set our tasks for them. As such, the images taken within the scope of photographs as analysis are a stepping stone towards familiarisation, a different kind of immersion into the data but also into the actual experiences of our participants. With that in mind, I would like to say quite explicitly that these photographs do not need to be shared. In most research reports or write-ups, we do not share all of our coding lists, sheets of analyses, screenshots of the coding information, or Post-it™ notes, either. In some cases, the photograph produced as an analytical process may be useful for the consumers of our research, or there may be a dissemination opportunity. The primary purpose of photographs as analysis, however, is not the sharing, but the sense-making.

The starting point for the analysis is therefore the participants' data, the pre-existing theories and knowledge, and, potentially, any analysis the researcher has done already. The end point is a photograph. How to get from the data starting point to the photograph end point is what makes this form of analysis difficult to describe. In effect, we engage in an intuitive, dynamic way, and we let ourselves be guided by our gut feelings and instincts. We then use the photograph as an opportunity to express our insights. It is the vagueness of this process that opens it up for criticism as not being scientific or systematic enough. And to an extent, I would agree. Where I disagree is with the assumption that the generation of codes and themes is less guided by instincts and gut feelings. There may be some codes that we glean from theories and publications. Many codes, however, we make up as we go along, and we call them 'open codes'. If we are honest

Figure 4.6: Clay person

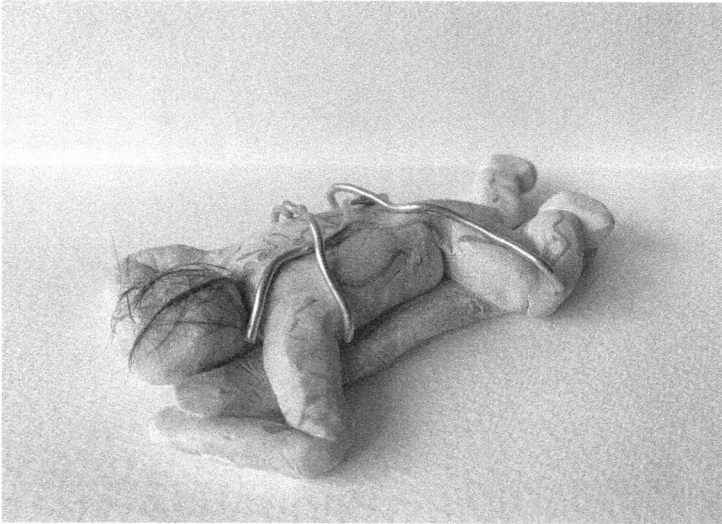

about what happens during analysis, open codes are nothing else but our instinctive labelling of sections of data that we respond to.

In order to untangle and demystify some of the vagueness with photographs as analysis and to show what the process may bring to research, I draw on my fibromyalgia work. The data I collected were interviews, photographs of identity boxes, fibromyalgia timelines from experiences of symptoms through to diagnosis, and curricula vitae. The sheer quantity and the vast variety of data felt overwhelming, and so I used different media to capture what I found essential. I built a clay figure that encapsulated some of the fibromyalgia symptoms if they were visible (see Figure 4.6). Many participants also talked about the value and benefit of nature, of going for walks, and of being on holidays, specifically for their mental health, but also to improve their symptoms due to the warmer climates, for example. So, I took photographs of outdoor spaces (see Figure 4.7).

Participants also talked quite openly about how they were missing their pre-diagnosis selves, how they grieved for what was and what is no longer, how they wanted to reconcile their fibromyalgia body with the good that travelling and nature bring.

Figure 4.7: Photograph of a field in Kent

Through organising and refining the photographs I had taken myself, I realised that the fibromyalgia bodies were forcing my participants to live in ways they would not necessarily have wanted for themselves. Instead of being able to do what they wanted to, participants seemed to somehow experience a trapped existence. I tried to capture that experience with the help of a sphere glass lens (see Figure 4.8).

Reading through the process here, it appears that this interpretation of being trapped in a body should have been quite straightforward. Being in the throes of data, facing the messiness of what was said and shared with me, I became so overwhelmed that I could not see the wood for the trees. Focusing on taking photographs as representations enabled me to step out of the many details, to take a more holistic view, and therefore to access my data in different ways. The photographs in themselves are quite meaningless now. At the time, they allowed me to connect with the experiences of my participants, and they helped me uncover themes. Maybe I would not have missed those themes; maybe I would have. In any case, the photographs as analysis offers space to (re)think. And even if there had not been any new insights

Figure 4.8: Photograph of clay person reflected in a sphere glass lens

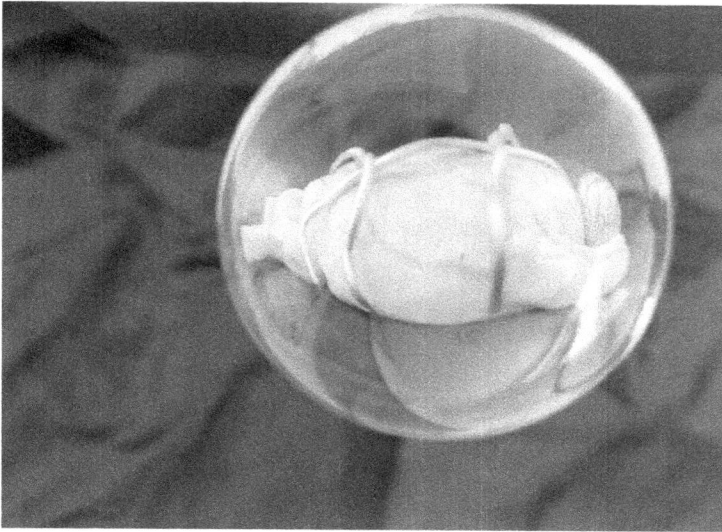

to be gained, the process itself was interesting and made analysis more enjoyable as well as manageable for me.

Participant involvement in analysis

Having spent considerable amount of space on the description of how to analyse photographs, I would like to return more explicitly to the context of photovoice, as so far, I have not focused on the role of the participants within the process of the analysis. To this end, I am returning to the reframing of photovoice presented in Chapters 1, 2, and 3, where I outlined photovoice as a framework, as it was originally designed, and photovoice as a method (see Figure 3.1 in Chapter 3). Photovoice as a framework is about community engagement from the outset and therefore requires the participants doing the analysis with the researcher merely facilitating that process (for further details, consider Liebenberg, 2018, 2022 and Liebenberg et al, 2020).

In practice, many researchers draw on the participatory elements that photovoice as a method offers. So, to then consider analysis purely from the researcher's position feels like an oversight.

Indeed, there are many publications about research using photovoice that report on having involved participants within the analytical processes.

For example, Tsang (2020) describes approaching photovoice from a participatory visual analysis standpoint. Accordingly, photographs are analysed based on the researcher's interpretations, but are also analysed based on the participants' interpretations, with the resulting findings then being cross-referenced and compared to one another. Along the continuum of participant engagement, this approach would then probably be located somewhere to the lower end of participant engagement, as the cross-referencing and final analyses are done by the researcher in independence of the participants. Similarly, Tümkaya et al (2021) refer to the participants' creation of captions and stories in relation to photographs. To the authors this is the participant involvement, as the participants engage in a first layer of interpretation within the analytical process. Tanhan and Strack's (2020) project would probably be located somewhere further to the right of the continuum of participant involvement, as the research team facilitated their participants' meaning-making process. Recognising that participants may feel out of depth during analysis, the researchers asked for the creation of captions and metaphors that effectively took the function of codes. At the far end of the continuum, I would place the work of Alison Finch (2023). For her doctoral research, Finch explored the experiences of ambulatory care among young people aged between 16 and 24 who had cancer. While this was not specifically designed as a study using photovoice as framework, her research design does share significant similarities with that approach. To then accommodate community involvement and foster agency, she worked with young adults to engage as co-researchers within every stage of the research, including the data collection phase and analysis. Together with Finch herself, a nurse, two parents, and a professional co-researcher, these young adults constituted the core participatory analysis team. Analysis then was a joint sense-making, in 'a co-researcher community and was conceptualised as a co-constructed endeavour', during which 'I did not feel I should be a leader among equals' (Finch, 2023, np). Similarly, the team around Professor Gasteiger-Klicpera from the University of Graz,

Austria, also emphasised the sense-making experience within the participant group. In their project on Mental Health Literacy and Diversity, young people aged between 12 and 15 from Austria, Slovenia, and Poland shared their photographs according to the SHOWeD technique (see Chapter 3) and were then required to cluster their photographs using Post-it™ notes (see project website at https://project.meheli-d.uni-graz.at/de/).

These publications demonstrate that the involvement of participants in photovoice analysis can take many forms. And it is possible to include participants' views in all three approaches presented in this chapter. The advantages of participant involvement are evident: increased accuracy, increased agency, increased community engagement, and increased relevance of the research. The main concerns around participant involvement relate to use of time and to the skill set required for the tasks. Finch (2023) spent significant time on training co-researchers, evaluating their experiences, and reviewing and refining their roles together with them. By contrast, Tanhan and Strack (2020), Tsang (2020), and Tümkaya et al (2021) worked with their participants' existing abilities to create stories, captions, and initial levels of interpretation. As researchers we just end up making decisions depending on our particular research contexts, and that may mean focusing on accuracy and authenticity in some cases, and on effective use of time in others.

End of chapter tasks

1. Return to the ten photographs you took in response to the task in Chapter 3. Using the guidelines on how to analyse photographs, try to immerse yourself in them, code them, and interpret them. Notice when you move from one stage to the next, and reflect on when and how you know that it is time to move on to the next stage. Use your journal to note your observations.

2. Access a data set in any format. If you have a data set you can use, draw on that. If you do not have an existing data set, register an account with *The Qualitative Data*

Repository at https://qdr.syr.edu and download a data set from their database. Familiarise yourself with the data to then create a photograph or a series of photographs representing the data you accessed. Then explore your photographs. Reflect on your process and consider what you gleaned from using photographs as analysis. Record your thoughts and reflections in your journal.

5

Photovoice and dissemination

Chapter aims

- To reflect on the role of dissemination as a pathway to impact.

- To introduce criteria for assessing the quality of photovoice research.

- To consider advantages and drawbacks of different ways to disseminate photovoice research.

Introduction

Having discussed the foundations and design of photovoice as well as different approaches to data collection and analysis, it is now time to turn to dissemination. Due to its emphasis on community engagement, photovoice as a framework builds in dissemination of findings from the design stages (see Chapters 2 and 3). However, even if research designed as photovoice as framework quite naturally lends itself to the sharing of findings, researchers and participants need to be aware of what it means to engage in disseminating photovoice. Also, research may take the form of photovoice as method. And in that case, dissemination requires extra planning.

Generally, photovoice research, whether it is designed as a framework or a method, has the purpose of benefiting society and communities and of bringing about change. The level of change and the level of participant engagement will depend on the specifics of a research project, but all research needs to be shared in some ways in order to benefit society, thus have impact. As stakeholders, such as grant funders, research institutions, and community organisations, look for evidence of the impact of a research project, the planning for research impact constitutes an important part of life as a researcher. This is where dissemination comes in. If a project is judged for its impact on society, thus the benefit the outcomes of the research bring, then dissemination is the pathway to that impact. There cannot be any impact of a research, if the findings of a research do not get shared. So, in order to understand the pragmatics of disseminating photovoice research, it is important to learn about impact, as it can take many forms. Within the context of academic publishing and research excellence, impact is often defined as

> an effect on, change or benefit to the economy, society, culture, public policy or services, health, the environment or quality of life, beyond academia. (UK Research and Innovation, 2022, para 1)

This definition often feels daunting for photovoice researchers, as the categories are too broad to be meaningful in studies that are often of a small scale. It may therefore be more helpful to think of impact differently. To improve research impact, as well as to gain the evidence required to demonstrate research impact, Reed (2018) recommends that researchers plan the engagement with relevant stakeholders from the outset. Although *The Research Impact Handbook* (Reed, 2018) does not specifically relate to photovoice research, the connections to photovoice as a framework are evident. In the case of photovoice as method, Reed's ten categories of impact and their respective definitions should prove useful:

1. **Understanding and awareness impacts:** people understand an issue better than they did before, based on your research.
2. **Attitudinal impacts:** a change in attitudes, typically of a group of people who share similar views, towards a new attitude that brings them or others benefits.

3. **Economic impacts:** monetary benefits arising from research, either in terms of money saved, costs avoided, or increases in turnover, profit, funding, or benefits to groups of people or the environment measured in monetary terms.

4. **Environmental impacts:** benefits from research to genetic diversity, species or habitat conservation, and ecosystems, including the benefits that humans derive from a healthy environment.

5. **Health and well-being impacts:** research that leads to better outcomes for the health of individuals, social groups, or public health, including saving lives and improving people's quality of life, and wider benefits for the well-being of individuals or social groups, including both physical and social aspects, such as emotional, psychological, economic well-being, and measures of life satisfaction.

6. **Policy impacts:** the contribution that research makes to new or amended laws, regulations, or other policy mechanisms that enable them to meet a defined need or objective that delivers public benefit. Crucial to this definition is the fact that you are assessing the extent to which your research made a contribution, recognising that it is likely to be one of many factors influencing policy.

7. **Other forms of decision-making and behaviour change impacts:** whether directly or indirectly (via changes in understanding/awareness and attitudes), research can inform a wide range of individual, group, and organisational behaviours and decisions, leading to impacts that go beyond the economy, environment, health, and well-being or policy.

8. **Cultural impacts:** changes in the prevailing values, attitudes, beliefs, discourse, and patterns of behaviour, whether explicit (for example, codified in rules or law) or implicit (for example, rules of thumb or accepted practices).

9. **Other social impacts:** benefits to specific social groups or society not covered by other types of impact.

10. **Capacity or preparedness:** research that leads to new or enhanced capacity (physical, financial, natural, human resources, or social capital and connectivity) that is likely to lead to future benefits, or that makes individuals, groups, or organisations more prepared and better able to cope with

changes that might otherwise impact negatively on them. (Adapted from Reed, nd, np)

Within the context of photovoice research in all its designs then, there is definitely scope for impact across all ten categories, even if economic, environmental, and health and well-being impacts may be somewhat more difficult to plan for. The key to achieving research impact with photovoice research is to see beyond academic publishing and to therefore engage with dissemination in different formats.

In the following, I begin with a focus on quality within photovoice research before considering the pragmatics of disseminating photovoice research through research publications and conference presentations, exhibitions, and dissemination events, and dedicated websites and social media platforms. I conclude the chapter with a consideration of the consequences of disseminating photovoice research.

Assessing the quality of photovoice research

Throughout the previous chapters, I mentioned benefits as well as pitfalls and critiques relating to photovoice research. I also hinted at the wider debate around quality within qualitative research, when I recommended that photovoice researchers should consider literature and publications from wider fields rather than their own disciplinary contexts only. As we now think about dissemination and the sharing of findings, it is necessary to return to some of these aspects. Assuming that our photovoice research is carried out to the highest possible standards of ethics and integrity, we can be reassured that our data collection is robust and rigorous, and that our analysis is compelling, coherent, and credible (for example, Hammersley, 2007; Tracy, 2010; Flick, 2018). However, when it comes to sharing research, we need to also be sure that our findings are meaningful and impactful. So, in order to be able to select data to be disseminated, we must learn how we can assess the quality of the work to be shared. Researchers using photovoice as method or as framework do so because of the power of the image as a 'can-opener' or 'golden key' (Collier and Collier, 1986, p 25) to experiences. Similarly, when it comes to dissemination, photographs function as tools to explain and justify analyses, along with their benefit to enable emotional connections among audiences. Thus, as researchers, we need to assess the value of photographs generated during the research. And to this end, we should draw upon criteria from frameworks that help evaluate the quality of art-based research.

Within the scope of art-based research, the researchers need to assess the quality of creative outputs and creations generated during research, very much like the photographs generated in photovoice research. However, not every creation is there to be shared. Above all, there is the question of intentionality. If a photograph was generated as an analytical process, then there is a different intention behind the image to the photograph taken for dissemination purposes. The image of the clay figure reflected in a sphere glass lens (see Figure 4.8) is a good example. The photograph developed as an analytical process and, as such, it was never intended for the public eye. But what if I had intended it as a public image, would it have stood up to scrutiny? Let us consider the image using some key criteria from art-based frameworks.

In addition to the typical criteria for quality in research, art-based frameworks refer to 'social significance' and 'evocation and illumination' (Barone and Eisner, 2011, pp 148–55) or 'audience response', 'aesthetics or artfulness', and 'personal fingerprint or creativity' (Leavy, 2015, pp 272–80). If I was to critically reflect on these criteria looking at the clay figure in the sphere glass lens, I would suggest that I probably met 'personal fingerprint or creativity' and 'social significance', but that I completely missed the mark for 'evocation and illumination' and 'aesthetics or artfulness'. The clay person on its own (see Figure 4.6) illuminates the experience of fibromyalgia and is artful in that evocation. But once I took the photograph of the clay figure reflected in the glass sphere, it somehow lost its evocative powers.

What then about 'audience response'? To gauge the effect my work would or could possibly have, I always share my photographs with my most trusted critics, members of my family, participants, peers, and colleagues. Only once I know that the work stands up to the quality criteria, I am confident to share my creations with relevant stakeholders. Consequently, much of what I produce remains in files on my computer, unused.

For my fibromyalgia research, I had at one point tried to connect the landscape images (see Figure 4.7) with the clay person in the glass sphere (see Figure 4.8). Figure 5.1 shows a draft of an image manipulated to express how nature and being outdoors remains elusive for many people with fibromyalgia.

When the initial audience response was something along the lines of "what is it with the chicken in the snow?", it was very clear that the intended message was not conveyed. Of course, I had known that this photograph (see Figure 5.1) was not my best creative piece, but honestly, I had not realised quite how far away from a meaningful representation I was. I had not planned on sharing the image as it was, at that stage, but I had planned on developing the idea further. This is the first time I am sharing the photograph, almost as a warning. Just because you have honed your creative juices, and just because you may have enjoyed the creative process of generating an image, it does not follow that the result is meant for sharing or wider use. Only what is of good quality should be considered for dissemination.

Figure 5.1: Photoshopped image to represent the experience of fibromyalgia

Pragmatics of disseminating of photovoice research

In line with there being many different forms of impact, there are equally many ways to tread the pathway to that impact, thus dissemination. In the following, I discuss advantages and concerns relating to the most typical pathways: research publications and conference presentations, exhibitions and dissemination events, and the sharing of information and data via dedicated websites, blogs, and social media platforms.

Research publications and conference presentations

Throughout this book, I have referred to articles that have been published in academic journals. This would not have been possible without researchers and participants disseminating their work in such publications. Unfortunately, as systematic reviews show (Hergenrather et al, 2009; Coemans et al, 2019; Derr and Simons, 2020; Suprapto et al, 2020), in many academic publications the original intention of photovoice as a framework to participant-led research remains elusive. Publication in journals fosters a researcher's credibility and standing, and is currency within the context of building and navigating a career in academia. Yet, as is widely acknowledged, research publications do not get read by the parties and stakeholders that matter when it comes to social change. Often, the articles are behind paywalls, which are barriers to independent research institutions, individuals, community organisations, and entire communities. Looking through academic publications relating to photovoice projects, another key factor becomes evident: photographs do not get published. With many publishing companies nowadays using physical copies along with accompanying online spaces, where articles are often made available long before they are assigned an actual volume, photographs have become a more common feature. However, it is not unheard of for an academic to be told that they would have to make a choice between reducing the word count of a written article in order to insert a picture and deleting the picture. In practice, writers need the space to explain and explore, to justify and argue, and so, unfortunately, images are then often pushed aside in favour of the written word. In addition, such articles are written to meet the criteria of academic conventions, which, in turn, means that the language used, theorisation employed, and the arguments put forward make the reading of the articles complex or irrelevant. In short, articles are inaccessible, literally as well as metaphorically speaking. Conference presentations are slightly less inaccessible in that regard, as researchers can adjust their presentations to suit their audiences, and there do not tend to be any rules about the use of images within presentation slide decks. However, the cost and nature of conferences remain a reason for relevant stakeholders and communities to feel out of their depths and to therefore not attend. To counteract prohibitive costs, many researchers resort to curating exhibitions and holding dissemination events.

Exhibitions and dissemination events

Dissemination events in the context of photovoice range from exhibitions, presentations, and talks to public appearances, media engagement, and other activities. In their project to give Latina '*mujeristas*' voice to proactively counter the marginalisation that Latina women experience, Mejia et al (2013) facilitated dissemination and public engagement via community radio stations and through outreach events and activities with individual research participants going on to become volunteers in schools and to continue activist work in their communities. Ronzi et al (2016) report on a curated photo-exhibition with a viewing event for stakeholders. The project originally explored older people's experiences and perceptions of respect and social inclusion in four geographical areas in Liverpool, UK. Ahead of the exhibition, participants were required to agree on a selection of 60 out of 127 photographs as well as on the captions for the photographs in the show. For the viewing event, perceived dignitaries, stakeholders, decision makers, and policy makers were invited, and speakers included representatives of the museum, academic institutions, and the mayoral office. During the event, some participants spontaneously engaged directly with visitors by explaining their photographs. Another study aimed at exploring health promoters' perceptions of housing issues among farm-working families in an agricultural community, while also focusing on subsequent strengthening of community capacity to promote affordable housing in the US (Postma and Ramon, 2016). This project is particularly noteworthy, as significant capacity- and community-building activities emerged. Initially, a multimedia video of 13 minutes in length was created in English and Spanish from photographs and interview footage. Participants shared the video widely to increase awareness. However, the video then also formed the basis for further activities, which included the development of a targeted network between health clinics, the mayoral office, and members of the city council to improve housing needs assessment and to promote healthy housing. The video also gained traction in the public eye with articles appearing in local, regional, and state newspapers, and the video itself having become a training resource to illuminate the experience of homelessness among children. This impact at community level eventually led to the state-level recognition of the video as an outcome of the photovoice research, which, in turn, helped shape the agenda for initiatives around healthy and affordable housing at state level.

These projects are great examples of the power of photovoice research once it is disseminated. Unfortunately, the dissemination work is not easy. Developing a video, curating an exhibition, organising an event − all of these activities require resources; specifically, they require time, money, skills, and contacts. If you have ever tried to edit a video or organise a conference you will already appreciate how much time, and money, is needed to be putting something together that is meaningful and impactful. It may therefore be better to organise a webinar, which can be advertised via an events management and ticketing service, and which can be held online using existing conference-call applications. Within the contemporary context, the most common applications are Eventbrite, Teams, and Zoom. Depending on the size and demographic of your target audience, however, you may want to manually organise the ticketing via a simple spreadsheet. It needs to be considered, though, that the benefit of an online webinar is at the same time its drawback: it is online. If the participants and/or the target audience are likely to have limited access to the internet, then a webinar is practically inaccessible. In-person exhibitions and events with discussion panels or presentations may therefore be more appropriate. If that is required for the context of your research, I suggest considering approaching local community organisations and charities, as well as funding agencies and institutions, for academic research. Both strands may enable you to access financial or material support. Maybe your local village hall would be happy to host your event, if they are able to sell teas, coffees, and cake. Maybe your local church would be happy to host your event, as part of their outreach and community engagement activities. Maybe research funders will see the potential impact of your study and will offer funding. Already, the need for contacts emerges. Not only will you need to be linked with local, regional, and potential national organisations to host your event, you will also need to be well connected to invite the relevant stakeholders. Policy makers, city council members, and representatives of mayoral offices will most likely be selective about the kinds of events they attend. Having created a network and being linked with the relevant stakeholders well ahead of your dissemination event is therefore a big advantage. With that, let me return to skills. There is a skill in networking and connecting ahead of an event; there is also a skill in following up on dissemination events and pursuing the participants' agenda further, as there is a skill in the development of photographs and videos.

For many researchers, this list may feel quite overwhelming. To that, let me just say, nobody does everything. With funding, there is an opportunity to write the technical and administrative support into a project from the start. But even where there is limited or no funding, there are possibilities. Local communities, local charities, even individuals, may be quite happy to support a worthy cause, if they are approached and asked. The worst that can happen when you ask for specific help is that the answer will be 'no'. Maybe, however, the answer is not an outright 'no', more a 'no, not now' or 'no, but'. So, instead of shying away from a dissemination plan entirely, maybe there is scope to rethink.

Dedicated websites, blogs, and social media platforms

Probably, the most common way to share photovoice research is via dedicated websites, blogs, and social media platforms. If you are interested in finding out more about photovoice projects,

I recommend checking out PhotoVoice. PhotoVoice is an organisation based in the UK that uses participatory photography for the purpose of social change. The charity's website offers ideas and resources, as well as training and a curation of photovoice projects that were set in the UK or overseas. The earliest registered project dates back to the 1990s, when PhotoVoice co-founder Tiffany Fairey began her anthropological fieldwork to Bhutanese refugee camps to support young Nepalese refugees who had entered Bhutan. The curated project list is available at https://photovoice. org/projects/. The team behind the 'Feeling at Home' project in the UK have taken a slightly different approach with their website. The site is a dedicated space to collate and share important information, news, and events details as they relate to the study. The aim of the research is to explore how people with learning disabilities experience the sense of feeling 'at home', and what helps or hinders them gain that sense of belonging and at-home-ness. The website then brings together the views of the researchers as project organisers with the experiences of co-researching participants who have led and facilitated some of the participant discussions, and with the participants directly through curating an online gallery of project-generated photographs. The participant-supplied photographs can be viewed in the online gallery at https://feelin gathome.org.uk/exhibition/. A similar website relates to the project 'Images of Incoming: a photovoice project exploring belonging and exclusion with newcomer and migrant women in rural areas', which involved around 70 women from Northern Ireland and Canada. The participant-generated photographs can be viewed as prints, as photographic records of a physical exhibition, and as a 4-minute video based on the physical gallery space (www.qub.ac.uk/ sites/photovoice/Exhibitions/). A 45-minute video documentary is also shared on the website, along with many more details about the project and its outcomes. The Mental Health Literacy and Diversity project also has a specific, dedicated space for sharing the photographs with captions that were generated in the photovoice study across Austria, Poland, and Slovenia (https://project.meheli-d.uni-graz.at/de/aktivitaten/partizipative-aktivitaten/).

In addition to the these more traditional online spaces, there are also online virtual galleries, such as Art.Spaces (https://artspa ces.kunstmatrix.com/en) or collaborative tools such as Padlet (https://en-gb.padlet.com/) that can be used. Art.Spaces is intended for artists, exhibitors, and curators, and enables individuals to develop high-quality 3D exhibitions of art, which can then be shared directly or embedded into websites. Rather than the sharing being focused on text, the emphasis is on the photographs. Padlet allows individuals to share their experiences through photographs, videos, as well as texts. For a collaborative project exploring identity and sense of belonging the visual artist, educator, and participatory photography facilitator Alejandra Carles-Tolra and I experimented with Padlet. We both took photographs in our respective environments sharing them on the padlet and then responded to each other's posts. We either linked to the posts directly, or added new photographs (see Figure 5.2).

Figure 5.2: Screenshot of Nicole and Alejandra's padlet exploring identity and sense of belonging

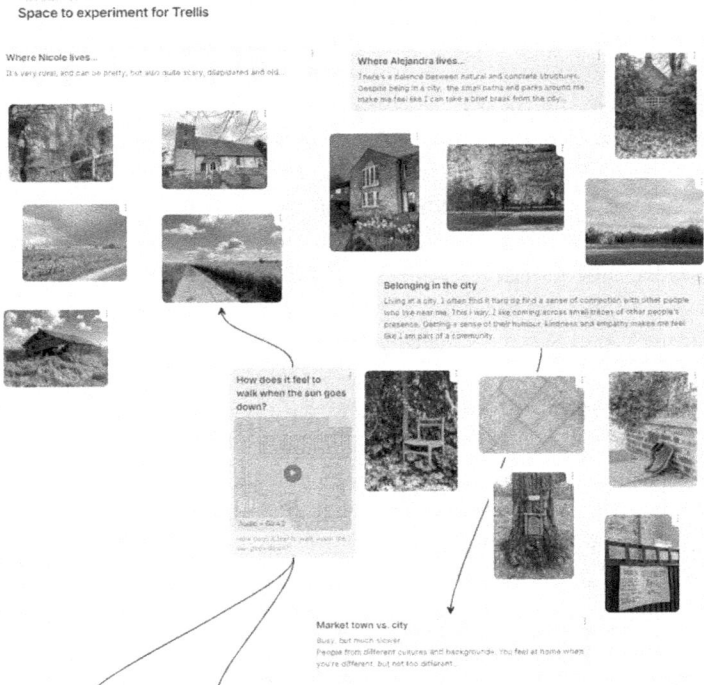

In a way, in our project, the padlet was a record of the process of data generation and analysis, while a more refined version of it could possibly also have been used for dissemination purposes. As a dissemination tool, the padlet could very simply be the virtual space where participants post their photographs to be shared. The padlet can then be shared directly or embedded into a more formal blog or website.

Organising and creating a website, blog, and/or some other social media platform, such as on YouTube, Facebook, or Instagram, is probably quite appealing, as the relevant websites and applications make the processes of sharing relatively easy and cost-effective. Of course, my earlier argument about access to the internet still stands. However, in many contexts and settings, participants and communities are engaging with websites and social media, and so, hosting an exhibition online is a natural extension of the in-person events, which enables much wider reach.

However, the practicalities of maintaining a website, blog, and/or social media platform are much rarely discussed or considered. A website, blog, and/or social media presence are only meaningful if they keep being revised, reviewed, refreshed, and updated. And this may be an important factor in the decision of what is shared on a website. For example, if a researcher is funded to carry out a photovoice study, then the website will probably be linked to that project for as long as the funding is active. Once the funding period ends, the researcher will most likely not have the capacity and means to continue maintaining the website. In fact, the researcher may move on to new projects with entirely different methodologies, even. As a result, the online presence stagnates.

Writing as someone who has maintained a professional website for the best part of a decade, I would say it is quite easy to create a website and a social media handle, it is less easy to then develop traffic onto those, it is more difficult to remain on the pulse of time, and it is much more complicated still to gain meaningful engagement from traffic to a website.

> While our core group of co-researchers worked hard to share our project through various social media outlets as well as through formal school channels, we were unable to get a feel for how the project

was taken up by those it reached. We could access numerical indicators related to how many social media accounts our outgoing messages may have reached, but without responses, the effectiveness of the dissemination was unclear. (Call-Cummings and Hauber-Özer, 2021, p 3223)

So, even with statistics offering details of how many visits to a site may have happened in what period, or of how many times a newsletter was opened, it is impossible to gauge actual reach or impact. With these realities in mind, we need to then ask ourselves if it is ethical and moral to share participants' photographs on websites, and how we may approach the topic of creating an online exhibition and/or website with our participants from the outset.

Consequences of disseminating photovoice research

This chapter on dissemination would not be complete without some reflections on the potential consequences of disseminating photovoice research (see also Chapter 6). Because of the power of photographs, dissemination activities often focus on the sharing of the images that are generated in the course of the study. However, this sharing may not be entirely unproblematic, as it fosters vulnerability among the creators, whether they are the researchers or the participants. If you have ever created an output to be shared, you will be aware of what it feels like to make yourself vulnerable to criticism and feedback. With images generated during photovoice research, there is unnatural pressure on the creators to nonetheless share their work, as the community engagement for social change is built into the framework. Are the participants truly able to say that they do not wish their photographs to be shown? Or is it that the vulnerability stemming from opening themselves up is the price to be paid to support social justice issues?

Vulnerability not only relates to the creative strands of the study. It also refers to technical aspects. Even if the images themselves appear relatively neutral and do not depict any identifiable details, there is information embedded in images which the photographers may be unaware of. All photographs contain a certain amount of such metadata. The International Press Telecommunications Council (IPTC), an international news media standards body based in the UK, distinguishes three categories of metadata:

> **Descriptive**: information about the visual content. This may include headline, caption, keywords. Further persons, locations, companies, artwork or products shown in the image. This can be done using free text or codes from a controlled vocabulary or other identifiers.
> **Rights**: identification of the creator, copyright information, credits and underlying rights in the visual content including model and property rights. Further rights usage terms and other data for licensing the use of the image.
> **Administrative**: creation date and location, instructions for the users, job identifiers, and other details. (IPTC, nd)

The metadata embedded in the image stays with the photograph for purposes around the rights of use, identification, and online tracking of use. The downside of these copyright protection measures is that the photographer may also be trackable through the details saved. Depending on the cameras and the settings being used during photography, the GPS details pinpointing to the exact location may be viewable. Due to the nature of photovoice research, by default photographs will be taken in participants' communities, but potentially even within their own homes, as for example in the 'Feeling at Home' project mentioned earlier. Using the photographs from our padlet (see Figure 5.2) in a reverse Google image search together with the metadata embedded in the images, it was possible to pinpoint where Alejandra and I lived. For us, this was an interesting exercise when we considered using Padlet for our own research project. Basically, unless the photographers, researchers, or web teams edit the embedded metadata, the privacy of the individuals involved in the project is in no way guaranteed.

Consequences of disseminating photovoice extend to the researcher in a slightly different way. Being a qualitative researcher taking a particular approach to data collection, analysis, and dissemination is a conscious choice. Engaging with photovoice as a framework or as a method is therefore quite a natural progression from the first choices taken. However, it may help to consider longer-term consequences. Using photovoice as method allows the researchers to navigate dissemination on their terms, which would most often revolve around publications and conferences, and possibly some form of dissemination via relatively static websites. In these circumstances, participants are often not included as equal leaders or team members, but as participants. In projects employing photovoice as a framework, however, the participants engage in, take responsibility for, and in most cases lead on dissemination activities. And the researcher, as a facilitator of these dissemination activities, enters the realm of policy development, public engagement, knowledge transfer, and activism.

When I was working on my fibromyalgia research, I always felt that I had a duty to do more than merely write publications. My participants spent significant amounts of time and energy on doing something entirely selfless, taking part in my research, and so, I felt, I needed to give something back. As this giving back could not be directly to each participant, I turned my energies on giving back to the higher education community more broadly. It was with that in mind that I organised a conference on 'Ableism in Academia', which was held in 2018, which, in turn, was the starting point for two edited books. I began formulating recommendations for practice to be shared in academic institutions to advocate for academics with disabilities, chronic illnesses, and/ or neurodivergence. I had no specific plan for my research work to turn into activism, but that is effectively what happened.

The question any budding photovoice researcher must ponder is: do you want to be an activist? Being an advocate or activist is as time-consuming and energy-draining as it is important, meaningful, and noble. For some researchers, the step into advocacy, public engagement, and policy development may just be a step too far. Of course, there is an opportunity to balance research work with involvement in advocacy and social justice issues, as it is possible to reinvent oneself and change emphasis along the way. It just needs to be said that the transformative nature of photovoice, especially of photovoice as a framework, does not begin and end with the participants or the stakeholders; it begins and ends with the researchers themselves.

End of chapter tasks

1. Return to the ten photographs you took and reduced to three in response to the task in Chapter 3, and which you analysed in Chapter 4. Using the information from this chapter, consider which of the ten – or three – photographs you would use for dissemination purposes and which dissemination activities you would engage in. What would be involved in setting up your preferred strands for dissemination? Use your journal to record your reflections and justifications.

2. Explore the metadata of your photographs. For this task, I suggest you use the ten photographs you took in Chapter 3, but also any personal photographs you may have on your devices. Depending on the devices you use, there will be different ways to access the metadata EXIF data embedded in your images. Google how to view the metadata on your device, and check out the kind of information that your photographs, and screenshots, contain. If you are happy to upload an image, you could also use one of the many free online EXIF viewers available, such as Metadata2Go, which is available at www.metadata2go.com/. In your journal, reflect on the data embedded in your photographs, what information you share, and what you can do to make the photograph less revealing.

Photovoice now and in the future

Chapter aims

- To reflect on ethical considerations in photovoice research.

- To offer guidance on how to manage ethics approvals processes.

- To demonstrate how photovoice research may be developed further.

Introduction

Throughout this book I focused on the foundations and historical development of photovoice, on how to design photovoice research, what data collection and analysis in photovoice research may look like, and what to consider when disseminating photovoice research. Although I have hinted at some ethical considerations around harm or vulnerability, I have so far not gone into detail regarding the ethics of photovoice research. I personally believe that ethics is a continual, relational process that needs to permeate an entire research project. However, based on my experiences in workshops, I decided to separate ethical considerations from other aspects of research design. In practice, this separation is artificial, and some ethical conundrums do impact the research design, which in turn leads to further reconsideration of the role and purpose of photovoice research.

This final chapter, therefore, has the dual purpose of tying up the missing strands and of staking out the future of photovoice. Hence, this chapter is backward- and forward-looking at the same time. It refers to the key aspects of photovoice as presented in this book with a view of how such research can be done ethically, and it highlights how the boundaries of these traditional conventions may be pushed further to widen the applications and uses of photovoice across disciplines.

I begin with a section on the ethics approval process, before considering in greater detail the role of photographs in photovoice research. I then explore issues of resources, time and effort, and concerns around anonymity and confidentiality. I conclude the chapter with a reflection on what further developments the future may bring for photovoice research.

Photovoice and the ethics approval process

In our contemporary social sciences landscape, there are many trends at play that impact our understanding of research and that shape research designs (Brown, 2022b). The current climate of casualisation and precarity in academia means individuals either engage in independent research or join research institutions outside of academia. At the same time, there is an increased interest in participatory approaches stemming from the need to 'decolonise' research and the need to develop an original contribution to wider scholarship. As a result, the uses of photovoice as a method and as a framework are also on the increase. Unfortunately, ethics approvals processes are not necessarily keeping up with these fast changes. For many institutions, and indeed publishers, ethics approvals processes are still a means to protect against legal claims and allegations of misconduct. Rather than seeing the ethics approvals process as an opportunity to foster academic integrity and ethical behaviour, the emphasis in ethics reviews often remains on protection and safeguarding of participants in order to ensure an institution does not come to any reputational or legal harm. Although I try not to be cynical, I cannot help but notice that many concerns workshop delegates bring to me in relation to ethics approvals processes for photovoice research stem from the circumstances I describe here. For example, in research using a photovoice as a framework, researchers will not know the exact research question to be investigated, nor will they know what kinds of activities will be developed during data collection, analysis, and dissemination. Yet, institutional review boards require these details for a study to gain ethics approval.

I strongly encourage staged or phased ethics applications, which I also use in my own institution. Effectively, I will apply for an initial, first ethics approval to go into the field and explore the circumstances with my participants. I am as accurate as possible with what kinds of activities I plan in order to create the circumstances required for my participants and me to jointly plan our project. Usually, this phase will include workshop-type activities or focus group discussions. It may not even be necessary to record this phase of the research, which essentially means there are hardly any contentious ethical issues. Once I have received approval for this first phase, I then do as I said I would to engage participants, communities, and stakeholders to define the next stages of the research. I then apply for an amendment to my original ethics application, an option that many institutions offer. In reality, this amendment is treated as a new application, and will undergo a full review. So even in institutions, where amendments to ethics approvals are not offered, researchers can apply for ethics approval for the next phase of their work. I repeat the process when my participants and I come to the point to decide on the details of dissemination activities. Unfortunately, when it comes to independent researchers or research institutions outside of academia, the ethics approval process is much more difficult. There are organisations willing to review ethics, such as for example the Aotearoa Research Ethics Committee (https://aotearoaresearchethics.org/) or the Social Research Association (https://the-sra.org.uk/SRA/SRA/Ethics/Ethics-appraisal-service.aspx). But in most cases, researchers will be asked to consider their approach to research in relation to existing ethics guidelines and frameworks, such as those from the British Educational Research Association, the Social Research Association, the American Psychological Association, the American Association for Public Opinion Research, or from the publishing companies. Let us therefore focus on some of the ethical considerations that we should reflect on in our work.

Photographs in photovoice research

It goes without saying that photovoice research relies on photographs, irrespective of whether they are researcher-supplied or participant-supplied, and whether they are found or generated. However, dealing with photographs, more specifically the taking of photographs, requires special consideration.

In Chapter 5, I mentioned that photographs can identify individuals and their locations from the embedded metadata. I would like to go in a little more detail here, as the metadata also lays out copyrights and rights of use. In Chapter 3, I described how Matteucci (2013) used found photographs, and that Allen (2020) emphasised the time-savings gained from using found rather than created photographs. Indeed, it may appear quite simple to for participants or researchers to search for photographs on the internet to use as found photographs. However, the use of found photographs is not quite as straightforward. Researchers and participants may not necessarily know which images they can access and use freely, and which images are protected and should not even be downloaded. There are image libraries that individuals can access and from where downloads are permitted for specific uses. But the choice of images is limited and there are costs involved in using these libraries. These issues are further complicated nowadays with the increased use of artificial intelligence. AI offers an opportunity for photographs to be created to such an artistic and realistic extent that it becomes nearly impossible to distinguish authentic images from artificial ones. In Spain, photographs displaying naked teenage girls were AI-generated from original images, where the girls had been fully clothed (Hedgecoe, 2023). The consequences from such cases are immense. However, the opportunity of AI-generated images, for which the laws around ownership, rights, and copyrights are not yet defined clearly enough, is enticing.

The consideration of ownership of the materials is also relevant when using participant-generated photographs. Superficially, the choice is simple. The materials belong to the participants, as they create and generate the photographs for the photovoice research. Yet, there is another argument: the photographs would not come into existence without the work of the researcher. Therefore, ownership of the photographs needs to be split unequally with the majority share belonging to the participants because they create the photographs, but the minority share belonging to the researcher, who has created the circumstances of the research and/or the prompts for the photographs. Whatever the ultimate arrangements are between researchers and participants, all parties need to be fully aware of how photographs may be used and/ or shared. For example, a researcher may want to use images in publications and at conferences, while the participant may want to use images on their websites. Together they will need to work out if the use in one context still allows for the use in other contexts, or if there will be restrictions. This is particularly important when it comes to photographs that participants create as an art form and may want to use them as an artistic documentation of lived experiences. Photography as an art form is hugely sellable, so research participants would be well within their right to create prints from their work to generate some income. Even if this route is not often pursued in photovoice research, the mere fact that the opportunities are there demonstrates the importance of having clear arrangements around ownership.

In photovoice research using participant-generated photographs, the matter of photographing, the physical act of taking a picture needs to be considered. Irrespective of how much experience participants may have with using cameras and taking photographs, there is a difference between snapping for personal reasons and generating images for research purposes. Researchers and participants ought to jointly develop the parameters for the taking of photographs. These specifications need to include details on who or what to take a photograph of and how to take that photograph ethically. This means that everyone involved in the photovoice research must be clear about the rules around consent. In artistic contexts, for example, photographers may take photographs covertly, then approach the person who is the subject of the photograph and ask for permission to keep the photograph. Australian photographer Jay Weinstein's 'So I asked them to smile' series builds on this exact premise. Weinstein takes a photograph of strangers, then asks them to smile for another picture. He then sets these images side by side. His work can be viewed on Instagram (www.instagram.com/soiaskedthemtosmile/) and on the website at www.soiaskedthemtosmile.com/. In the context of research, we must ask ourselves if taking a photograph covertly is ethical, even if consent is sought immediately. Exploring the boundaries and circumstances of covert research more broadly, Davey Calvey highlights that the current, predominant ethical perspective 'views covert research as violating the principle of informed consent' (Calvey, 2017a, p 8). However, he further outlines how the issue with covert research is not necessarily linked with 'extreme or high-risk environments' (Calvey, 2017b, p 50) and that therefore ethical considerations as well as risk around covert research may have been overestimated somewhat. Maybe, therefore, it is not unethical to take photographs of others within the realm of 'opportunistic possibilities (…) in public spaces and places' (Calvey, 2017b, p 50) without asking for consent immediately, and maybe in some such situations consent is not required at all before the photograph is taken. At the same time, it is important to recognise the impact of such a decision. For a researcher it may sound easy to stipulate that the photovoice research participants must seek consent from the people in their photographs before the picture is taken. However, as Novek et al (2012) report from their experiences with photovoice research:

> reluctance on the part of some older persons to ask permission, and to have others sign forms, was discernible. (Novek et al, 2012, p 464)

The authors then go on to highlight that, in the end:

> only 8 per cent of photos had identifiable people in them; only 19 consents were obtained, out of a total of 393 photos. (Novek et al, 2012, pp 464–5)

The need to approach strangers, the formality of asking for consent, and the formality of requiring a signature are all contributors to why photovoice research participants may struggle with this aspect of taking photographs. Novek et al (2012) also report that many of their research participants felt verbal consent would be sufficient, as the photographs were of family and friends rather than strangers. In any case, one consequence of the stipulation to ask consent is that photovoice research participants take their photographs differently. They avoid taking images that would otherwise be deemed pertinent. The fact that participants may view the taking of the photographs in a specific way needs to be considered a little more.

Without diving into a discussion into whether photographs can and do depict the truth, we can generally acknowledge that they are a depiction and representation. And therein lies the crux. For me, writing from an Anglo-Eurocentric viewpoint, photographs as representations are largely unproblematic. Yet, there are cultures and societies, for whom a photograph, thus the creation of the representation, is not unproblematic at all. For Amish people, for example, a photograph draws attention to the individual, which goes against their belief in community values and the relevance of community (Moneymaker, nd). By contrast, according to the photographer Jay Weinstein, individuals in rural villages in China and India take great care of what they look like before a photograph is taken, as they see the photography as an important event (Muzdakis, 2021). The issue of stereotyping on the one hand, while on the other hand not considering cultural specificities sufficiently, is well critiqued within the context of research relating to and representations of Indigenous peoples (Higgins, 2014). In short, it is important to remember that individuals associated with specific cultures and societies may have strong feelings about photography that differ from their cultural views. But it is also crucial to appreciate cultural specificities and consider how these will impact on the use of photographs within the context of data collection, analysis, and dissemination.

Resources, time, and effort

In publications, researchers mention how time-consuming photovoice research is, and that it is best to always plan more time than you think you need, especially where the design is that of photovoice as a framework (Allen, 2020; Brickley, 2022). In fact, most participatory research tends to take longer, simply because of the logistics of organising meetings, coming together, planning together, and taking decisions together. However, if we are to do photovoice research ethically, we should not consider how much of *our* time the research takes. Instead, we ought to focus on our participants, on how much of *their* time is required, on how many of *their* resources will be used, and on how much of *their* effort we are asking for. The more resources, time, and effort we demand, the more we need to give back. If our research requires participants to be involved as co-researchers, then, surely, we cannot step away from engaging in some of the activist work that truly begins during the dissemination phase of the research, thus once the research is finished.

Anonymity and confidentiality

In connection with the time and effort that we are asking participants to spend on our photovoice projects, I would like to mention anonymity and confidentiality. In many contexts of social sciences research, there is an endeavour to ensure that participants remain anonymous. The endeavour is noble and well meant, yet, may not be workable or desirable, even. I have mentioned how photographs may identify individuals from the metadata or from what is depicted, and I have hinted at how some of these details can be edited to avoid making research participants vulnerable. However, the need for anonymity and confidentiality may be misguided. As research participants in photovoice as framework projects are involved in or even lead dissemination activities (for example, Mejia et al, 2013; Ronzi et al, 2016; Postma and Ramon, 2016), the participants' rights to anonymity and confidentiality become automatically waived. In the context of photovoice as a method, there are opportunities to navigate rights to anonymity and confidentiality. In my workshops, I often hear how researchers would like to enable the waiving of anonymity and confidentiality to ensure that individuals' voices may be heard and that individuals may take formal and public ownership over their contributions, thus the photographs they generate. However, I hear equally often how ethics approvals processes require researchers to insist on anonymity and confidentiality. I do not know about all institutional review boards and ethics committees, and so I may not be able to solve this issue. Yet, I would like to point out that there are ethics guidelines that may constitute helpful justifications for arguing against anonymity and confidentiality:

in some circumstances individual participants, or their guardians or responsible others, may want to specifically and willingly waive their right to confidentiality and anonymity: researchers should recognise participants' rights to be identified in any publication of their original works or other inputs if they so wish. (BERA, 2018, p 21, item 40)

This excerpt from the British Educational Research Association ethics guidelines (2018) demonstrates very clearly that anonymity and confidentiality do not have to be imposed at all. Unfortunately, with this section being presented as the second part of a clause written to impose anonymity and confidentiality, it often gets lost. In my own work, I often argue that I do not have the right to ownership of images and that therefore I also do not have the right to decide on how these materials are presented. If, therefore, participants would like to have their names attached to their photographs, I make sure that they understand the repercussions as becoming formally named participants in my research. For some participants, this is not an issue; for others this is a concern, as they may not have disclosed their disability, chronic illness, and/or neurodivergence in public, for example. I then navigate the ethics around naming and not naming, around waiving and not waiving the right to anonymity and confidentiality with each participant separately throughout the different stages of the research.

Photovoice research in the future

Throughout this book, I focused on photovoice as a framework and photovoice as a method. This distinction is useful to identify similarities and differences between photovoice and photo elicitation. This reimagining of photovoice also helps to see where photovoice research is headed. In no way do I wish to confound terminologies or water down research designs. I do, however, recognise that particular ways of working, especially within the funding arena and institutional ethics reviews settings, have already had an impact and that such trends are bound to continue. Rather than stopping these dynamic developments of research methods,

I suggest we address them head-on, so that photovoice research is carried out deliberately, not haphazardly, and well, not poorly.

With the popularity of handheld devices unstoppable and the technological achievements being equally unfaltering, it is only a question of time for photovoice to turn into a form of videovoice. Video elicitation interviews (for example, Li and Ho, 2019; Colliers et al, 2020; Kanovský et al, 2020) and video journals (for example, Walker and Boyer, 2018; Taylor et al, 2019; Villamizar and Mejía, 2019) are already widely used within the context of data collection. Of course, the use of videos instead of photographs during data collection, analysis, and dissemination will require different ethical, methodological, and practical thought processes. But the step from video-making as a research method to video-making as a framework is not massive.

Technological advancements also continue to make it easier for individuals to undertake their own editing in photo and video software programmes. As a result, photoshopped or even AI-generated visual materials will lead to different, renewed forms of image creation and generation. As has already been touched upon, the use of AI specifically will require their own ethics considerations around ownership, anonymity, confidentiality, rights of use, and copyrights.

Photovoice is also closely aligned with and linked to material methods, and therefore these two approaches could easily be combined. Material methods are:

1. routes *into* the substantive field of materiality (even as the methods are simultaneously always part of that field), as well as
2. methods of researching *with* things (Woodward, 2020, p 2).

Instead of limiting data to interviews and/or photographs, material methods use objects as a means of communicating experiences and understanding the world. In many ways, some of the examples I discussed in this book are already touching upon this form of research, as they are using objects in that context of sense-making. If we were to push the boundaries further, photovoice research could therefore extend to object work or model-building. Participants could be asked to build models using materials from clay and Plasticine™ to LEGO® or to create assemblages with objects. These creations would then be photographed as per the usual approaches to photovoice.

The value of photovoice as participatory research for the purposes of social change is undisputed. Unfortunately, as we have seen, much completed photovoice research is not quite as emancipatory or transformative as it could be. This is to do not only with there being a lack of evaluation of social change, but also with there being flaws in the research design, where researchers do not consider dissemination as integral to photovoice research. Photovoice as a framework is well documented, and so does not require any changes to its foundational principles. It just needs researchers to carry out photovoice research as intended. Photovoice as a method, however, would benefit from further reimagining. And Fricas (2022) offers a way in. In her research the author investigated how Andean Indigenous notions of well-being influenced community health and participatory development in Ecuador. In her article, she argues that for photovoice research to be egalitarian, as well as contextualised meaningfully, it requires an anti-colonial stance, as that means:

> photovoice co-researchers can interrogate power differentials, question knowledge production and validation, and consider the options available in terms of agency, resistance, and refusal. (Fricas, 2022, p 4)

In her publication, Fricas (2022) highlights that by remaining 'ahistorical' in its philosophical foundation, photovoice research often perpetuates historical tendencies and colonial positionings. Instead of reiterating colonialisation, it is our duty as photovoice researchers to elevate Indigenous knowledge in such a way that we push back 'against the politics of knowledge subversion' (Dei and Lordan, 2016, p xiii). For me personally, this is probably the most exciting avenue to further develop photovoice. By asking us to engage more fully with the history and politics of colonialism, I can see how photovoice as a method could relatively quickly become an approach to research that would address our need for decolonising research methods. Therefore, instead of photovoice as a method being treated as the poor relation to photovoice as a framework or creative methods, the focus on an anti-colonial stance would turn photovoice as a method into its very own framework.

With that, let me end this chapter by returning to the beginning. I do not see photovoice as a framework and photovoice as a method as superior or inferior research designs. Photovoice as a framework and photovoice as a method are both powerful approaches to research with different theoretical foundations and philosophical outlooks leading to different research designs and therefore resulting in different outcomes. As times move on, our understanding changes, our knowledge develops, and there will always be opportunities to then develop these existing frameworks, foundations, and outlooks further. And that is desirable. However, I do strongly encourage researchers to engage with the historical and foundational principles to learn how to meaningfully apply the purist versions of photovoice, and to learn how to justify any deviations.

End of chapter tasks

1. Return to the previous end of chapter tasks, where you supplied and created photographs, and reflect on the ethical considerations raised in this chapter. Journal about the issues of vulnerability, anonymity, and confidentiality, and the time and effort you were required to input.

2. Look up Figure 3.1 'Photovoice reimagined' in Chapter 3 and consider where you can realistically situate your research, given the circumstances, settings, and contexts you are working within. Analyse the strengths, weaknesses, opportunities, and threats for undertaking your project as a photovoice as a method and as a photovoice as a framework. Record your thoughts in your journal.

References

Abrams, J. A., Tabaac, A., Jung, S., & Else-Quest, N. M. (2020). Considerations for employing intersectionality in qualitative health research. *Social Science and Medicine*, 258, 113138.

Allen, L. (2020). Schools in focus: photo methods in educational research. In: M. R. Ward & S. Delamont (eds). *Handbook of Qualitative Research in Education*. Cheltenham: Edward Elgar, pp 248–56.

Alvariza, A., Mjörnberg, M., & Goliath, I. (2020). Palliative care nurses' strategies when working in private homes—a photo-elicitation study. *Journal of Clinical Nursing*, 29(1–2), 139–51.

Anne, E. P. (2013). Ethnographic strategies for engaging deaf youth participants: photovoice and participatory analysis. *Student Anthropologist*, 3(3), 34–46.

Barone, T. & Eisner, E. W. (2011). *Arts-Based Research*. Thousand Oaks, CA: Sage.

Barry, J., Monahan, C. H., Ferguson, S. A., Lee, K, Kelly, R., Monahan, M. et al (2021). 'I came, I saw, I conquered': reflections on participating in a PhotoVoice project. *Journal of Mental Health Training, Education and Practice*, 16(4), 257–68.

BERA (British Educational Research Association) (2018). *Ethical Guidelines for Educational Research*, 4th edn, London. Available at: www.bera.ac.uk/researchers-resources/publications/ethi cal-guidelines-for-educational-research-2018. (Last accessed: 29 November 2023).

Blinn, L. & Harrist, A. W. (1991). Combining native instant photography and photo-elicitation. *Visual Anthropology*, 4(2), 175–92.

Bonisteel, I., Shulman, R., Newhook, L. A., Guttmann, A., Smith, S., & Chafe, R. (2021). Reconceptualizing recruitment in qualitative research. *International Journal of Qualitative Methods*, 20, 16094069211042493.

Bostock, L. (1997). *The Greater Perspective: Protocol and Guidelines for the Production of Film and Television on Aboriginal and Torres Straight Islander Communities.* Special Broadcasting Service. 2nd edn. Available at: www.wipo.int/export/sites/www/tk/en/databases/creative_heritage/docs/lester_bostock_film.pdf. (Last accessed: 28 September 2023).

Brackley, K. (2022). *Six Things We Learnt from our Photovoice Groups.* Available at: https://feelingathome.org.uk/blog/six-things-we-learnt-from-our-photovoice-groups/. (Last accessed: 28 September 2023).

Braun, V. & Clarke, V. (2011). *Successful Qualitative Research: A Practical Guide for Beginners.* London: Sage.

Breny, J. M. & McMorrow, S. L. (2020). *Photovoice for Social Justice: Visual Representation in Action.* Thousand Oaks, CA: Sage.

Brisolara, S. (2014). Feminist theory: its domains and applications. In: S. Brisolara, D. Seigart, & S. SenGupta, (eds). *Feminist Evaluation and Research: Theory and Practice.* New York, NY: Guilford Publications, pp 3–41.

Brown, N. (2022a). Research ethics in a changing social sciences landscape. *Research Ethics.* https://doi.org/10.1177/17470161221141011

Brown, N. (2022b). Scope and continuum of participatory research. *International Journal of Research & Method in Education,* 45(2), 200–11.

Brown, N. (2023). *Photovoice.* National Centre for Research Methods online learning resource. Available at: www.ncrm.ac.uk/resources/online/all/?id=20817. (Last accessed: 28 September 2023).

Brown, N. & Collins, J. (2021). Systematic visuo-textual analysis: a framework for analysing visual and textual data. *Qualitative Report,* 26(4), 1275–90.

Budig, K., Diez, J., Conde, P., Sastre, M., Hernán, M., & Franco, M. (2018). Photovoice and empowerment: evaluating the transformative potential of a participatory action research project. *BMC Public Health,* 18(1), 1–9.

Bunster, X. (1977). Talking pictures: field method and visual mode. *Signs: Journal of Women in Culture and Society,* 3(1), 278–93.

Burleigh, C. L., Wilson, A. M., & Lane, J. F. (2022). COVID-19: teacher interns' perspectives of an unprecedented year. *Qualitative Report,* 27(6), 1582–1606.

Cabassa, L. J., Nicasio, A., & Whitley, R. (2013a). Picturing recovery: a photovoice exploration of recovery dimensions among people with serious mental illness. *Psychiatric Services*, 64(9), 837–42.

Cabassa, L. J., Parcesepe, A., Nicasio, A., Baxter, E., Tsemberis, S., & Lewis-Fernández, R. (2013b). Health and wellness photovoice project: engaging consumers with serious mental illness in health care interventions. *Qualitative Health Research*, 23(5), 618–30.

Cahnmann-Taylor, M. & Siegesmund, R. (2018). *Arts-Based Research in Education*. 2nd edn. Abingdon: Routledge.

Caldarola, V. J. (1985). Visual contexts: a photographic research method in anthropology. *Studies in Visual Communication*, 11(3), 33–53.

Call-Cummings, M. & Hauber-Özer, M. (2021). Virtual photovoice: methodological lessons and cautions. *Qualitative Report*, 26(10), 3214–33.

Calvey, D. (2017a). Debates about covert research. In: D. Calvey (ed). *Covert Research: The Art, Politics and Ethics of Undercover Fieldwork*. London: Sage. https://doi.org/10.4135/9781473920 835, pp 1–19.

Calvey, D. (2017b). Doing covert research in the social sciences. In: D. Calvey (ed). *Covert Research: The Art, Politics and Ethics of Undercover Fieldwork*. London: Sage. https://doi.org/10.4135/ 9781473920835, pp 1–50.

Carlson, E. D., Engebretson, J., & Chamberlain, R. M. (2006). Photovoice as a social process of critical consciousness. *Qualitative Health Research*, 16(6), 836–52.

Carter, B. & Ford, K. (2013). Researching children's health experiences: the place for participatory, child-centered, arts-based approaches. *Research in Nursing & Health*, 36(1), 95–107.

Catalani, C. & Minkler, M. (2010). Photovoice: a review of the literature in health and public health. *Health Education & Behavior*, 37(3), 424–51.

Chapman, M. V., Wu, S., & Zhu, M. (2017). What is a picture worth? A primer for coding and interpreting photographic data. *Qualitative Social Work*, 16(6), 810–24.

Chen, S. H. (2011). Power relations between the researcher and the researched: an analysis of native and nonnative ethnographic interviews. *Field Methods*, 23(2), 119–35.

Clements, K. (2012). Participatory action research and photovoice in a psychiatric nursing/clubhouse collaboration exploring recovery narrative. *Journal of Psychiatric and Mental Health Nursing*, 19(9), 785–91.

Close, H. (2007). The use of photography as a qualitative research tool. *Nurse Researcher*, 15(1), 27–36.

Coemans, S., Raymakers, A. L., Vandenabeele, J., & Hannes, K. (2019). Evaluating the extent to which social researchers apply feminist and empowerment frameworks in photovoice studies with female participants: a literature review. *Qualitative Social Work*, 18(1), 37–59.

Collier, J. (1957). Photography in anthropology: a report on two experiments. *American Anthropologist*, 59(5), 843–59.

Collier, J. & Collier, M. (1986). *Visual Anthropology: Photography as a Research Method*. Albuquerque, NM: University of New Mexico Press.

Colliers, A., Coenen, S., Bombeke, K., Remmen, R., Philips, H., & Anthierens, S. (2020). Understanding general practitioners' antibiotic prescribing decisions in out-of-hours primary care: a video-elicitation interview study. *Antibiotics*, 9(3), 115.

Cook, T. & Hess, E. (2007). What the camera sees and from whose perspective: fun methodologies for engaging children in enlightening adults. *Childhood*, 14(1), 29–45.

Curry, T. J. (1986). A visual method of studying sports: the photo-elicitation interview. *Sociology of Sport Journal*, 3(3), 204–16.

Dahlberg, K., Dahlberg, H., & Nyström, M. (2011). *Reflective Lifeworld Research*. 2nd edn. Lund: Studentlitteratur.

Dei, G. J. S. & Lordan, M. (2016). Introduction: envisioning new meanings, memories and actions for anti-colonial theory and decolonial praxis. In: G. J. S. Dei & M. Lordan (eds). *Anti-Colonial Theory and Decolonial Praxis*. New York, NY: Peter Lang.

Derr, V. & Simons, J. (2020). A review of photovoice applications in environment, sustainability, and conservation contexts: is the method maintaining its emancipatory intents?. *Environmental Education Research*, 26(3), 359–80.

Dowdall, G. W. & Golden, J. (1989). Photographs as data: an analysis of images from a mental hospital. *Qualitative Sociology*, 12(2), 183–213.

Evans-Agnew, R. A. (2018). Asthma disparity photovoice: the discourses of black adolescent and public health policymakers. *Health Promotion Practice*, 19(2), 213–21.

Evans-Agnew, R. A. & Rosemberg, M. A. S. (2016). Questioning photovoice research: whose voice?. *Qualitative Health Research*, 26(8), 1019–30.

Ewald, W. (1985). *Portraits and Dreams: Photographs and Stories by Children of the Appalachians*. New York, NY: Writers and Readers Publications.

Feighey, W. (2003). Negative image? Developing the visual in tourism research. *Current Issues in Tourism*, 6(1), 76–85.

Finch, A. (2023). *Experiences of Teenage and Young Adult Ambulatory Care: Community-Based Participatory Research to Inform Service Provision* [Unpublished doctoral thesis]. London: University College London.

Flick, U. (2018). *Managing Quality in Qualitative Research*. Vol 10. London: Sage.

Foster-Fishman, P., Nowell, B., Deacon, Z., Nievar, M. A., & McCann, P. (2005). Using methods that matter: the impact of reflection, dialogue, and voice. *American Journal of Community Psychology*, 36(3), 275–91.

Freire, P. (2017). *Pedagogy for the Oppressed*. London: Penguin Modern Classics.

Freire, P. (2021). *Education for Critical Consciousness*. London: Bloomsbury Publishing.

Fricas, J. (2022). Towards an anticolonial photovoice: a research practice guide to theoretical and methodological considerations. *Journal of Participatory Research Methods*, 3(2).

Friedman, D. B., Foster, C., Bergeron, C. D., Tanner, A., & Kim, S. H. (2015). A qualitative study of recruitment barriers, motivators, and community-based strategies for increasing clinical trials participation among rural and urban populations. *American Journal of Health Promotion*, 29(5), 332–8.

Given, L. M., Opryshko, A., Julien, H., & Smith, J. (2011). Photovoice: a participatory method for information science. *Proceedings of the American Society for Information Science and Technology*, 48(1), 1–3.

Gleeson, K. (2011). Polytextual thematic analysis for visual data. In: P. Reavey (ed). *Visual Methods in Psychology: Using and Interpreting Images in Qualitative Research*. Hove: Taylor & Francis, pp 314–29.

Grange, H. & Lian, O. S. (2022). 'Doors started to appear': a methodological framework for analyzing visuo-verbal data drawing on Roland Barthes's classification of text–image relations. *International Journal of Qualitative Methods*, 21. https://doi.org/10.1177/16094069221084433

Groot, B. C., Schrijver, J., & Abma, T. A. (2021). Are You Afraid of Press and Social Media? Ethics in Photovoice in Participatory Health Research. *Educational Action Research*, 31(3), 556–74.

Hammersley, M. (2007). The issue of quality in qualitative research. *International Journal of Research & Method in Education*, 30(3), 287–305.

Han, C. S. & Oliffe, J. L. (2016). Photovoice in mental illness research: a review and recommendations. *Health*, 20(2), 110–26.

Harley, D., Hunn, V., Elliott, W., & Canfield, J. (2015). Photovoice as a culturally competent research methodology for African Americans. *Journal of Pan African Studies*, 7(9), 31–41.

Harper, D. (2002). Talking about pictures: a case for photo elicitation. *Visual Studies*, 17(1), 13–26.

Harper, D. (2005). An argument for visual sociology. In: J. Prosser (ed). *Image-Based Research: A Sourcebook for Qualitative Researchers*. London: Routledge, pp 24–41.

Hatten, K., Forin, T. R., & Adams, R. (2013). A picture elicits a thousand meanings: photo elicitation as a method for investigating cross-disciplinary identity development. In: *2013 ASEE Annual Conference & Exposition*, 23891–238921.

Hedgecoe, G. (2023). AI-generated naked child images shock Spanish town of Almendralejo. *BBC* [online]. Available at: www.bbc.co.uk/news/world-europe-66877718. (Last accessed: 28 September 2023).

Hergenrather, K. C., Rhodes, S. D., Cowan, C. A., Bardhoshi, G., & Pula, S. (2009). Photovoice as community-based participatory research: a qualitative review. *American Journal of Health Behavior*, 33(6), 686–98.

Hidalgo Standen, C. (2021). The use of photo elicitation for understanding the complexity of teaching: a methodological contribution. *International Journal of Research & Method in Education*, 44(5), 506–18.

Higgins, M. (2014). Rebraiding photovoice: methodological métissage at the cultural interface. *Australian Journal of Indigenous Education*, 43(2), 208–17.

Hubbard, J. (1991). *Shooting Back: A Photographic View of Life by Homeless Children*. Chronicle Books.

Hurworth, R., Clark, E., Martin, J., & Thomsen, S. (2005). The use of photo-interviewing: three examples from health evaluation and research. *Evaluation Journal of Australasia*, 4(1–2), 52–62.

Husserl, E. (1960). *Cartesian Meditations: An Introduction to Phenomenology*. The Hague: Springer.

IPTC. (nd). *What Is Photo Metadata? Definition, Types, and Relevance*. www.iptc.org/standards/photo-metadata/photo-metadata/. (Last accessed: 28 September 2023).

James, F. & Shaw, P. (2022). Finding the balance: the choreography of participatory research with children and young people. *International Journal of Research & Method in Education*, 46(4), 329–41.

Jarldorrn, M. (2019). *Photovoice Handbook for Social Workers: Method, Practicalities and Possibilities for Social Change*. Cham: Springer.

Kaaristo, M. (2022). Everyday power dynamics and hierarchies in qualitative research: the role of humour in the field. *Qualitative Research*, 22(5), 743–60.

Kane, J. (2004). *Culturally Sensitive Photography: Like Travel Itself, Photography Builds Bridges. Culturosity.com* [online]. Available at: https://cgi.unc.edu/wp-content/uploads/2017/09/culturally-sensitive-photography.original.pdf. (Last accessed: 28 September 2023).

Kanovský, M., Baránková, M., Halamová, J., Strnádelová, B., & Koróniová, J. (2020). Analysis of facial expressions made while watching a video eliciting compassion. *Perceptual and Motor Skills*, 127(2), 317–46.

Kara, H. (2015). *Creative Research Methods in the Social Sciences: A Practical Guide*. Bristol: Policy Press.

Kara, H. (2020). *Creative Research Methods: A Practical Guide*. 2nd edn. Bristol: Policy Press.

Knowles, J. G. & Cole, A. L. (2008). *Handbook of the Arts in Qualitative Research: Perspectives, Methodologies, Examples, and Issues.* Thousand Oaks, CA: Sage.

Kong, T. M., Kellner, K., Austin, D. E., Els, Y., & Orr, B. J. (2015). Enhancing participatory evaluation of land management through photo elicitation and photovoice. *Society & Natural Resources,* 28(2), 212–29.

Kortegast, C., McCann, K., Branch, K., Latz, A. O., Kelly, B. T., & Linder, C. (2019). Enhancing ways of knowing: the case for utilizing participant-generated visual methods in higher education research. *Review of Higher Education,* 42(2), 485–510.

Král, J. (1956). The use of aerial photographs & aerial ethnography in the study of rural settlement & rural economy. *Revista Geográfica,* 19(45), 16.

Kurtz, H. E. & Wood, J. (2014). Stone soup: photo-elicitation as a learning tool in the food geography classroom. *Journal of Geography in Higher Education,* 38(4), 546–56.

Lakoff, G. & Johnson, M. (2003). *Metaphors We Live By.* 2nd edn. Chicago, IL: University of Chicago Press.

Latz, A. O. (2017). *Photovoice Research in Education and Beyond: A Practical Guide from Theory to Exhibition.* New York, NY: Routledge.

Latz, A. O. & Mulvihill, T. M. (2017). *Photovoice Research in Education and Beyond: A Practical Guide from Theory to Exhibition.* New York, NY: Routledge.

Leavy, P. (2015). *Method Meets Art: Arts-Based Research Practice.* 2nd edn. New York, NY: Guilford Publications.

Leavy, P. (2020). *Method Meets Art: Arts-Based Research Practice.* 3rd edn. New York, NY: Guilford Publications.

Leavy, P. (ed) (2018). *Handbook of Arts-Based Research.* New York, NY: Guilford Publications.

Leigh, J. & Brown, N. (2021). *Embodied Inquiry: Research Methods.* London: Bloomsbury Publishing.

Lewin, K. (1946). Action research and minority problems. *Journal of Social Issues,* 2(4), 34–46.

Li, B. Y. & Ho, R. T. H. (2019). Unveiling the unspeakable: integrating video elicitation focus group interviews and participatory video in an action research project on dementia care development. *International Journal of Qualitative Methods,* 18, https://doi.org/10.1177/1609406919830561.

Lichty, L., Kornbluh, M., Mortensen, J., & Foster-Fishman, P. (2019). Claiming online space for empowering methods: taking photovoice to scale online. *Global Journal of Community Psychology Practice*, 10(3), 1–26.

Liebenberg, L. (2018). Thinking critically about photovoice: achieving empowerment and social change. *International Journal of Qualitative Methods*, 17(1). https://doi.org/10.1177/16094 06918757631

Liebenberg, L. (2022). Photovoice and being intentional about empowerment. *Health Promotion Practice*, 23(2), 267–73.

Liebenberg, L., Jamal, A., & Ikeda, J. (2020). Extending youth voices in a participatory thematic analysis approach. *International Journal of Qualitative Methods*, 19. https://doi.org/10.1177/16094 06920934614

Lindhout, P., Teunissen, T., & Reniers, G. (2021). What about using photovoice for health and safety? *International Journal of Environmental Research and Public Health*, 18(22), 11985.

Linton, R. (1990). Towards a feminist research method. In: A. Jagger & S. Bordo (eds). *Gender/Body/Knowledge*. New Brunswick, NJ: Rutgers University Press, pp 273–92.

Loeffler, T. A. (2004). A photo elicitation study of the meanings of outdoor adventure experiences. *Journal of Leisure Research*, 36(4), 536–56.

Machin, D. (ed) (2014). *Visual Communication*. Vol 4. Berlin: Walter de Gruyter.

Machin, D. & Ledin, P. (2018). *Doing Visual Analysis: From Theory to Practice*. Thousand Oaks, CA: Sage.

Maguire, P. (1987). *Doing Participatory Research: A Feminist Approach*. Amherst, MA: The Center for International Education, School of Education, University of Massachusetts.

Mahruf, M., Shohel, C., & Howes, A. (2007). Transition from nonformal schools: learning through photo elicitation in educational fieldwork in Bangladesh. *Visual Studies*, 22(1), 53–61.

Margolis, E. & Pauwels, L. (eds) (2011). *The SAGE Handbook of Visual Research Methods*. Thousand Oaks, CA: Sage.

Matteucci, X. (2013). Photo elicitation: exploring tourist experiences with researcher-found images. *Tourism Management*, 35, 190–7.

Mayorga-Gallo, S. & Hordge-Freeman, E. (2017). Between marginality and privilege: gaining access and navigating the field in multiethnic settings. *Qualitative Research*, 17(4), 377–94.

Mead, M. (1975). Worth and Adair: *Through Navajo Eyes: An Exploration of Film Communication and Anthropology. Studies in Visual Communication*, 2(2), 122–4.

Mejia, A. P., Quiroz, O., Morales, Y., Ponce, R., Chavez, G. L., & Torre, E. O. Y. (2013). From madres to mujeristas: Latinas making change with Photovoice. *Action Research*, 11(4), 301–21.

Mental Health Literacy and Diversity (nd). Available at: https://project.meheli-d.uni-graz.at/de/. (Last accessed 28 September 2023).

Meo, A. I. (2010). Picturing students' habitus: the advantages and limitations of photo-elicitation interviewing in a qualitative study in the city of Buenos Aires. *International Journal of Qualitative Methods*, 9(2), 149–71.

Messaris, P. & Gross, L. (1977). Interpretations of a photographic narrative by viewers in four age groups. *Studies in Visual Communication*, 4(2), 99–111.

Milne, E. J. & Muir, R. (2020). Photovoice: a critical introduction. In: L. Pauwels & D. Mannay (eds). *The SAGE Handbook of Visual Research Methods*. 2nd edn. Thousand Oaks, CA: Sage: pp 282–96.

Minthorn, R. S. & Marsh, T. E. (2016). Centering indigenous college student voices and perspectives through photovoice and photo-elicitation. *Contemporary Educational Psychology*, 47, 4–10.

Mitchell, C. (2011). *Doing Visual Research*. London: Sage.

Moneymaker, W. (nd). *Culture, Permission and Photography*. Available at: www.moneymakerphotography.com/culture-per mission-photography/. (Last accessed: 28 September 2023).

Muzdakis, M. (2021). Before and after photos reveal how much a smile changes a person's aura. [Interview]. Available at: https://mymodernmet.com/so-i-asked-them-to-smile-jay-weinstein/. (Last accessed: 28 September 2023).

Mysyuk, Y. & Huisman, M. (2020). Photovoice method with older persons: a review. *Ageing & Society*, 40(8), 1759–87.

Newington, L. & Metcalfe, A. (2014). Factors influencing recruitment to research: qualitative study of the experiences and perceptions of research teams. *BMC Medical Research Methodology*, 14, 1–11.

Niessen, S. A. (1991). More to it than meets the eye: photo-elicitation amongst the Batak of Sumatra. *Visual Anthropology*, 4(3–4), 415–30.

Novek, S., Morris-Oswald, T., & Menec, V. (2012). Using photovoice with older adults: some methodological strengths and issues. *Ageing & Society*, 32(3), 451–70.

Oliffe, J. L. & Bottorff, J. L. (2007). Further than the eye can see? Photo elicitation and research with men. *Qualitative Health Research*, 17(6), 850–8.

Panazzola, P. & Leipert, P. (2013). Exploring mental health issues of rural senior women residing in southwestern Ontario, Canada: a secondary analysis photovoice study. *Rural and Remote Health*, 13(2), 1–13.

Pauwels, L. (2010). Visual sociology reframed: an analytical synthesis and discussion of visual methods in social and cultural research. *Sociological Methods & Research*, 38(4), 545–81.

Pauwels, L. (2015). 'Participatory' visual research revisited: a critical-constructive assessment of epistemological, methodological and social activist tenets. *Ethnography*, 16(1), 95–117.

Pauwels, L. (2020). *Respondent-Generated Image Production*. Thousand Oaks, CA: SAGE.

Pauwels, L. & Mannay, D. (eds) (2019). *The SAGE Handbook of Visual Research Methods*. 2nd edn. Thousand Oaks, CA: Sage.

PhotoVoice (nd). Statement of ethical practice. Available at: https://photovoice.org/wp-content/uploads/2017/05/Ethical-Statement.pdf. (Last accessed: 28 September 2023).

Pink, S. (2021). *Doing Visual Ethnography*. 4th edn. London: Sage.

Plunkett, R., Leipert, B. D., & Ray, S. L. (2013). Unspoken phenomena: using the photovoice method to enrich phenomenological inquiry. *Nursing Inquiry*, 20(2), 156–64.

Poku, B. A., Caress, A. L., & Kirk, S. (2019). The opportunities and challenges of using photo-elicitation in child-centered constructivist grounded theory research. *International Journal of Qualitative Methods*, 18, 1609406919851627.

Postma, J. & Ramon, C. (2016). Strengthening community capacity for environmental health promotion through photovoice. *Public Health Nursing*, 33(4), 316–24.

Power, E. M. (2003). De-centering the text: exploring the potential for visual methods in the sociology of food. *Journal for the Study of Food and Society*, 6(2), 9–20.

Pullman, M. E. & Robson, S. (2006). A picture is worth a thousand words: using photo-elicitation to solicit hotel guest feedback. *CHR Tool No. 7*. Available at: https://ecommons.corn ell.edu/bitstream/handle/1813/71281/A_Picture_Is_Worth_a _Thousand_Words.pdf

Pyle, A. (2013). Engaging young children in research through photo elicitation. *Early Child Development and Care*, 183(11), 1544–58.

Radley, A. & Taylor, D. (2003). Images of recovery: a photo-elicitation study on the hospital ward. *Qualitative Health Research*, 13(1), 77–99.

Reed, M. (2018). *The Research Impact Handbook*. 2nd edn. Huntley: Fast Track Impact.

Reed, M. (nd). Fast Track Impact: what types of impact are there? Available at: www.fasttrackimpact.com/what-types-of-impact-are-there-subp. (Last accessed: 28 September 2023).

Reinharz, S. (1992). The principles of feminist research: a matter of debate. In: C. Kramarae & D. Spender (eds). *The Knowledge Explosion Generations of Feminist Scholarship*. New York NY: Teacher College Press, pp 423–37.

Ritchie, J., Lewis, J., Nicholls, C. M., & Ormston, R. (eds) (2014). *Qualitative Research Practice: A Guide for Social Science Students and Researchers*. 2nd edn. London: Sage.

Ronzi, S., Pope, D., Orton, L., & Bruce, N. (2016). Using photovoice methods to explore older people's perceptions of respect and social inclusion in cities: opportunities, challenges and solutions. *SSM – Population Health*, 2, 732–45.

Rose, G. (2023). *Visual Methodologies: An Introduction to Researching with Visual Materials*. 5th edn. London: Sage.

Rosen, D., Goodkind, S., & Smith, M. L. (2011). Using photovoice to identify service needs of older African American methadone clients. *Journal of Social Service Research*, 37(5), 526–38.

Rosler, M. (1989). In, around, and afterthoughts. In: R. Bolton (ed). *The Contest of Meaning: Critical Histories of Photography*. Cambridge, MA: MIT Press, pp 303–42.

Sanon, M. A., Evans-Agnew, R. A., & Boutain, D. M. (2014). An exploration of social justice intent in photovoice research studies from 2008 to 2013. *Nursing Inquiry*, 21(3), 212–26.

Savi, L. (2020). *Bags Inside Out*. London: V&A Publishing.

Scarry, E. (1985). *The Body in Pain: The Making and Unmaking of the World*. Oxford: Oxford University Press.

Schwartz, D. (1989). Visual ethnography: using photography in qualitative research. *Qualitative Sociology*, 12(2), 119–154.

Seitz, C. M. & Orsini, M. M. (2022). Thirty years of implementing the photovoice method: insights from a review of reviews. *Health Promotion Practice*, 23(2), 281–8.

Shaffer R. (1984). *Beyond the Dispensary: On Giving Community Balance to Primary Health Care*. Nairobi: African Medical Research Foundation. Available at: www.amoshealth.org/wp-content/uploads/sites/62/2019/10/Beyond-the-Dispensary.pdf. (Last accessed: 28 September 2023).

Shaw, P. A. (2021). Photo-elicitation and photo-voice: using visual methodological tools to engage with younger children's voices about inclusion in education. *International Journal of Research & Method in Education*, 44(4), 337–51.

Sikkens, E., van San, M., Sieckelinck, S., Boeije, H., & De Winter, M. (2017). Participant recruitment through social media: lessons learned from a qualitative radicalization study using Facebook. *Field Methods*, 29(2), 130–9.

Smith, D. E. & Ziller, R. C. (1977). A phenomenological utilization of photographs. *Journal of Phenomenological Psychology*, 7(2), 172–82.

Snyder, E. E. & Kane, M. J. (1990). Photo elicitation: a methodological technique for studying sport. *Journal of Sport Management*, 4(1).

Sontag, S. (2003). *Regarding the Pain of Others*. London: Penguin.

Spence, J. (1995). *Cultural Sniping: The Art of Transgression*. London and New York: Routledge.

Spencer, S. (2010). *Visual Research Methods in the Social Sciences: Awakening Visions*. Abingdon: Routledge.

Stamps III, A. E. (1990). Use of photographs to simulate environments: a meta-analysis. *Perceptual and Motor Skills*, 71(3), 907–13.

Stokrocki, M. (1985). Photographic analysis, elicitation, and interpretation as ways of understanding art teaching in a multicultural setting. *Journal of Cultural Research in Art Education*, 3(1), 56.

Strack, R. W., Magill, C., & McDonagh, K. (2004). Engaging youth through photovoice. *Health Promotion Practice*, 5(1), 49–58.

Styring, K. (2007). *In Your Purse: Archaeology of the American Handbag*. Bloomington, IN: AuthorHouse.

Suprapto, N., Sunarti, T., Wulandari, D., Hidayaatullaah, H. N., Adam, A. S., & Mubarok, H. (2020). A systematic review of photovoice as participatory action research strategies. *International Journal of Evaluation and Research in Education*, 9(3), 675–83.

Sutton-Brown, C. A. (2014). Photovoice: a methodological guide. *Photography and Culture*, 7(2), 169–85.

Tandon, R. (1988). Social transformation and participatory research. *Convergence*, 21(2), 5.

Tanhan, A. & Strack, R. W. (2020). Online photovoice to explore and advocate for Muslim biopsychosocial spiritual wellbeing and issues: ecological systems theory and ally development. *Current Psychology*, 39(6), 2010–25.

Taylor, A. M., van Teijlingen, E., Ryan, K. M., & Alexander, J. (2019). 'Scrutinised, judged and sabotaged': a qualitative video diary study of first-time breastfeeding mothers. *Midwifery*, 75, 16–23.

Tracy, S. J. (2010). Qualitative quality: eight 'big-tent' criteria for excellent qualitative research. *Qualitative Inquiry*, 16(10), 837–51.

Trombeta, G. & Cox, S. M. (2022). The textual-visual thematic analysis: a framework to analyze the conjunction and interaction of visual and textual data. *Qualitative Report*, 27(6), 1557–74.

True, G., Davidson, L., Facundo, R., Meyer, D. V., Urbina, S., & Ono, S. S. (2021). 'Institutions don't hug people:' a roadmap for building trust, connectedness, and purpose through photovoice collaboration. *Journal of Humanistic Psychology*, 61(3), 365–404.

Tsang, K. K. (2020). Photovoice data analysis: critical approach, phenomenological approach, and beyond. *Beijing International Review of Education*, 2(1), 136–52.

Tümkaya, S., Kayiran, B. K., Tanhan, A., & Arslan, Ü. (2021). Using online photovoice (OPV) to understand youths' perceptions of distance education during COVID-19. *International Journal of Education and Literacy Studies*, 9(4), 45–60.

UK Research and Innovation. (2022). *How Research England Supports Research Excellence: REF Impact*. Available at: www.ukri. org/about-us/research-england/research-excellence/ref-imp act/. (Last accessed: 28 September 2023).

Van Auken, P. M., Frisvoll, S. J., & Stewart, S. I. (2010). Visualising community: using participant-driven photo-elicitation for research and application. *Local Environment*, 15(4), 373–88.

Van Leeuwen, T. & Jewitt, C. (eds) (2001). *The Handbook of Visual Analysis*. London: Sage.

van Wijk, E. (2014). Recruitment and retention of vulnerable populations: lessons learned from a longitudinal qualitative study. *Qualitative Report*, 19(28).

Vassenden, A. & Jonvik, M. (2022). Photo elicitation and the sociology of taste: a review of the field, empirical illustrations, arguments for a 'return to photography'. *Sociological Quarterly*, 63(1), 154–74.

Villamizar, A. G. & Mejía, G. (2019). Fostering learner autonomy and critical reflection through digital video-journals in a university foreign language course. *Reflective Practice*, 20(2), 187–200.

Walker, E. B. & Boyer, D. M. (2018). Research as storytelling: the use of video for mixed methods research. *Video Journal of Education and Pedagogy*, 3(1), 1–12.

Wallerstein, N. (1987). Empowerment education: Freire's ideas applied to youth. *Youth Policy*, 9(11), 11–15.

Wang, C. & Burris, M. A. (1994). Empowerment through photo novella: portraits of participation. *Health Education Quarterly*, 21(2), 171–86.

Wang, C. & Burris, M. A. (1997). Photovoice: concept, methodology, and use for participatory needs assessment. *Health Education & Behavior*, 24(3), 369–87.

Wang, C., Burris, M. A., & Ping, X. Y. (1996). Chinese village women as visual anthropologists: a participatory approach to reaching policymakers. *Social Science & Medicine*, 42(10), 1391–400.

Wang, C. C. (1998). Practice notes: strategies in health education. Project: photovoice involving homeless men and women of Washtenaw County, Michigan. *Health Education and Behaviour*, 25(1), 9–10.

Wang, C. C. (1999). Photovoice: a participatory action research strategy applied to women's health. *Journal of Women's Health*, 8(2), 185–92.

Wang, C. C. & Pies, C. A. (2004). Family, maternal, and child health through photovoice. *Maternal and Child Health Journal*, 8(2), 95–102.

Wang, C. C. & Redwood-Jones, Y. A. (2001). Photovoice ethics: perspectives from Flint photovoice. *Health Education & Behavior*, 28(5), 560–72.

Wang, Q. & Hannes, K. (2014). Academic and socio-cultural adjustment among Asian international students in the Flemish community of Belgium: a photovoice project. *International Journal of Intercultural Relations*, 39, 66–81.

Warne, M., Snyder, K., & Gillander Gådin, K. (2013). Photovoice: an opportunity and challenge for students' genuine participation. *Health Promotion International*, 28(3), 299–310.

Werremeyer, A., Skoy, E., Burns, W., & Bach-Gorman, A. (2020). Photovoice as an intervention for college students living with mental illness: a pilot study. *Mental Health Clinician*, 10(4), 237–43.

Whiting, L. S. (2015). Reflecting on the use of photo elicitation with children. *Nurse Researcher*, 22(3).

Williams, M. & Moser, T. (2019). The art of coding and thematic exploration in qualitative research. *International Management Review*, 15(1), 45–55.

Willson, G. & McIntosh, A. (2010). Using photo-based interviews to reveal the significance of heritage buildings to cultural tourism experiences. In: G. Richards & W. Munsters (eds). *Cultural Tourism Research Methods*. Wallingford: Cabi, pp 141–55.

Wolbert, B. (2000). The anthropologist as photographer: the visual construction of ethnographic authority. *Visual Anthropology*, 13(4), 321–43.

Woodward, S. (2020). *Material Methods: Researching and Thinking with Things*. Thousand Oaks, CA: Sage.

Worth, S. & Adair, J. (1972). *Through Navajo Eyes: An Exploration in Film Communication and Anthropology*. Bloomington, IN: Indiana University Press.

Zurba, M., Tennent, P., & Woodgate, R. L. (2017). Worth a thousand words?: advantages, challenges and opportunities in working with photovoice as a qualitative research method with youth and their families. *Forum Qualitative Sozialforschung/ Forum: Qualitative Social Research*, 18(1), 22.

Index

References to figures and photographs appear in *italic* type; those in **bold** type refer to tables.